THE FURNESS WAY

Companion to this volume

1983 THE WESTMORLAND WAY

THE FURNESS WAY

by

Paul Hannon

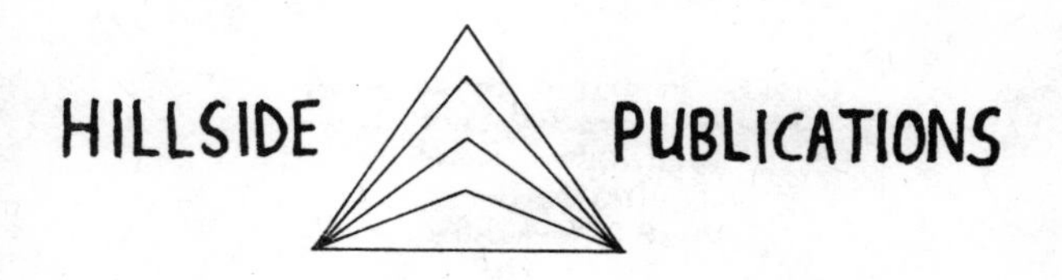

HILLSIDE PUBLICATIONS
11 Nessfield Grove
Exley Head
Keighley
West Yorkshire
BD22 6NP

Cover illustration: The Coniston Fells from Top O'Selside
Page 2: The Arms of the Stricklands of Sizergh

ISBN 0 9509212 1 1

Printed in Great Britain by
Joseph Ward Printers Ltd
Wellington Road
Dewsbury
West Yorkshire
WF13 1HR

CONTENTS

Arnside

Ravenglass

The Furness Way – the route and the six stages

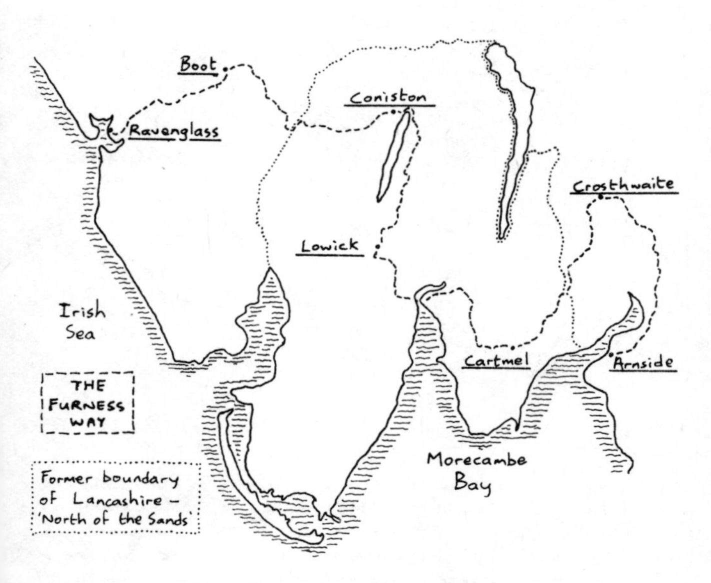

INTRODUCTION

This book is a guide to a 75 mile walk across southern lakeland, commencing at Arnside on the eastern side of Morecambe Bay, and finishing at Ravenglass, looking out to the Irish Sea. The Furness Way has been devised as a route to cross the southern part of Cumbria, whilst taking in as much as possible of the old county of Lancashire, north of the sands.

The main portion of this once detached section of Lancashire has been known for centuries as Furness, and no doubt will continue to be, particularly the lower lands south of the Lake District proper. To complete the old county is the Cartmel peninsular to the east, a Furness in miniature.

The Furness Way - physical features

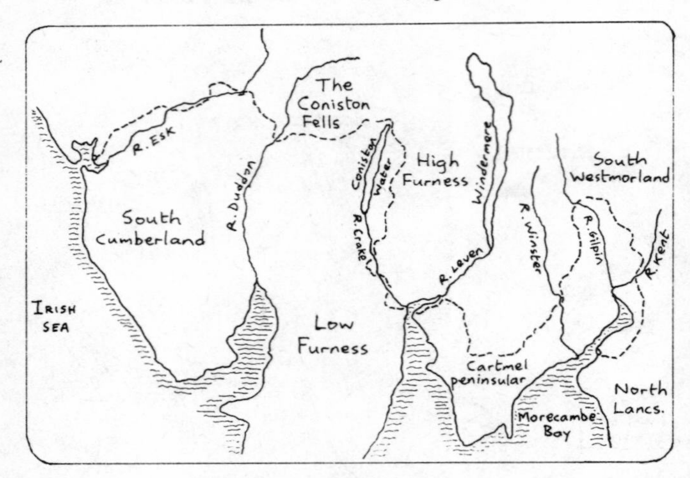

Despite it's allegiance to Furness, the walk actually begins in the old county of Westmorland and finishes in old Cumberland, both snatching a substantial part of the walk. However, the 'Southern Cumbrian Way' doesn't have quite the same ring to it! Incidentally, on this occasion I will desist from grumbling about chopping and changing the counties, for it has to be said that the Furness area seems more appropriate to the Cumbrian scene than the county palatine, for more reasons than it's physical detachment.

The Furness Way is, by and large, a relatively easy walk as long-distance routes go, and my recommendation that the 75 miles be divided into six daily sections ensures a fairly modest average of 12½ miles per day. This is unlikely to be too short for most walkers, as there are many ups and downs and plenty of interest along the way. The terrain is incredibly varied, from wide estuaries to mountain passes, and incorporating most other things in between these two extremities.

Returning from the romantic to the practical, each of the seven suggested overnight halts ends at a location providing accomodation of some kind, an indication of which I shall proceed to give. The two largest communities of Arnside and Coniston have plentiful bed and breakfast establishments, and both also possess youth hostels. Of the others, both Cartmel and Ravenglass have a handful of bed and breakfasts, while Crosthwaite, Lowick and Boot are all somewhat limited. The latter however, has a youth hostel and several accomodating farmhouses within very easy reach. Crosthwaite, Lowick Green and Lowick Bridge all possess at least one b+b, with one or two more within a mile or so. Both Crosthwaite and Lowick are also on bus routes that lead in only a short distance to Kendal/Bowness and Ulverston/Coniston respectively. At the top end of the scale, everywhere but Crosthwaite possesses a hotel where rather more expensive nights can be spent.

I am loath to include a list of addresses in a guide such as this as Mrs. Pitchfork on that cosy farm may suddenly decide she's seen more than enough bacon and eggs and is going to call it a day. What I do suggest is reference to the Ramblers Association B+B guide, which although covering the whole of Britain still contains many useful addresses. Less useful is the Tourist Board's 'Where to Stay' guide, which is a lavish production which is unfortunately extremely limited, consisting largely of colour advertisements.

As regards transport to and from the terminal points, both Arnside and Ravenglass have their own railway stations and are, as it happens, the only two met on the whole route. Both are connected to Carnforth on the main west coast line. Arnside is the first call on the Furness line to Barrow, which then heads north along the Cumbrian coast line to Carlisle, Ravenglass being sited part way along. Because of the relative inaccessibility of Ravenglass, British Rail is far and away the best transport to use, the service being quite regular and the opportunity to purchase a return ticket to Carnforth being useful.

Incidentally, if this six-day route leaves one with a day to spare, I would unreservedly recommend spending it in the same location as the fifth night of the walk. This way a heavy load could be abandoned for the day, and a walk amidst positively the finest mountain scenery in England would be possible, around the headwaters of the Esk.

As in my previous offering I shall devote a few lines to traditional beer. This corner of Cumbria can boast only one brewery, Hartleys of Ulverston, and even they are now in the hands of a larger brewer. Apart from their substantial hold on the local market, the other brewers represented hail from further afield, and are more sparsely spread. Jennings, Youngers and Vaux come from further north, the two national giants Bass and Whitbread show their colours, and the Lancashire brewers of Thwaites, Yates and Jacksons and Wilsons also put in brief appearances. Happily, on the Furness Way, there is very little to avoid.

Ordnance Survey maps required

These maps are essential companions on any walk, and will ideally complement this guide. What's more, only two need be carried.

1: 50,000 metric scale

sheet 96: South Lakeland
sheet 97: Kendal and Morecambe

1 inch to the mile

sheet 88: Barrow-in-Furness
sheet 89: Lancaster and Kendal

Early closing and Market Days

There is only one market, at Milnthorpe on Fridays

Early closing days are as follows:

Arnside - Thursday
Milnthorpe - Thursday
Cartmel - Thursday
Coniston - Wednesday

SOME USEFUL ADDRESSES

The Ramblers Association
1/5 Wandsworth Road, London SW8 2LJ
Tel. 01-582 6878

Youth Hostels Association
Trevelyan House, St. Albans, Herts. AL1 2DY
Tel. 0727-55215
Regional Office: Elleray, Windermere
Tel. Windermere (09662) 2301/2

Friends of the Lake District
Secretary: J.M. Houston, Gowan Knott, Kendal Rd, Staveley, nr. Kendal LA8 9AP
Tel. Kendal (0539) 821201

Cumbria Tourist Board
Ashleigh, Windermere LA23 2AQ
Tel. Windermere (09662) 4444

Ribble Motor Services
Bus Station, Blackhall Rd, Kendal
Tel. Kendal (0539) 20932
Head Office: Frenchwood Ave., Preston PR1 4LU
Tel. Preston (0772) 54754

The National Trust
36 Queen Anne's Gate, London SW1H 9AS
Tel. 01-222 9251
Membership: P.O. Box 30, Beckenham, Kent BR3 4TL
Tel. 01-650 7263

Campaign for Real Ale
34 Alma Rd, St. Albans, Herts AL1 3BW
Tel. 0727-67201

Lake District Weather Forecast - Tel. Windermere (09662) 5151

THE COUNTRY CODE

Respect the life and work of the countryside

Protect wildlife, plants and trees

Keep to public paths across farmland

Safeguard water supplies

Go carefully on country roads

Keep dogs under control

Guard against all risks of fire

Fasten all gates

Leave no litter - take it with you

Make no unnecessary noise

Leave livestock, crops and machinery alone

Use gates and stiles to cross fences, hedges and walls

THE ROUTE GUIDE

The maps in this guide again take the form of one continuous strip-map, which is spread over many pages, from page 17 to page 87. These maps are all to be found on right-hand pages, and each one has its point of continuation clearly indicated. On the same or facing page will be found a detailed commentary on the route depicted on that map. What space remains is filled with notes and drawings of places of interest along the way. Each section commences with an introductory page.

The maps are all on the scale of 2½ inches to the mile, and the top of the page is always north.

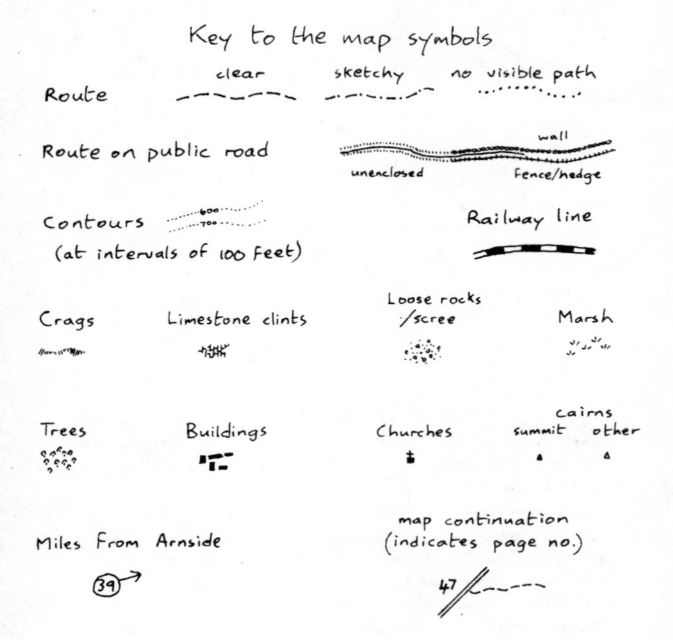

DAY ONE — ARNSIDE TO CROSTHWAITE

Distance - 15 miles

Going - easy

Highest point - Helsington Church, 425 feet

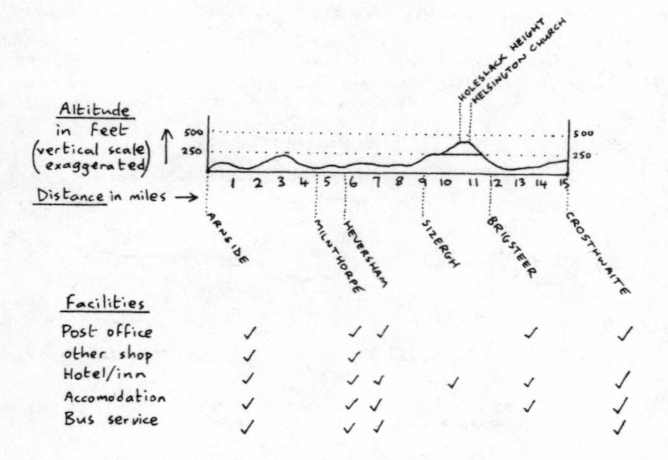

Facilities

	Arnside	Milnthorpe	Heversham	Sizergh	Brigsteer	Crosthwaite
Post office	✓	✓	✓		✓	✓
other shop	✓	✓				
Hotel/inn	✓	✓	✓	✓	✓	✓
Accomodation	✓	✓	✓		✓	✓
Bus service	✓	✓	✓			✓

The first day is also the longest day, though the distance is hardly overfacing in view of the mild nature of the terrain. It is, in fact, a veritable cultural extravaganza. Passed en route are some splendid old buildings, from the ruinous pele at Hazelslack to the grandeur of Sizergh Castle, Dallam Tower and Levens Hall. The Way also takes in the serene parkland of the latter two, along with fine views from the modest heights of Holeslack and Helsington Church

The front,
Arnside

Arnside, already well-favoured as the finishing point of the 98 mile-long Westmorland Way, is now furthering it's acquaintance with long-distance walks, as the resort now plays host to the 75 mile-long Furness Way. With one route ending and a new one starting here, surely nothing more could be asked of it?

Always a bright and breezy community, Arnside stands on the shoreline of Morecambe Bay, where the waters of the River Kent merge into it. There are no gaudy seaside entertainments here, just attractions that are strictly natural. The exception to this is the mighty Kent viaduct, which carries the railway to Furness over 50 arches high above the estuary. A train pulling out of the station always attracts the interest of visitors, who will watch it chug over every arch.

Above the houses rises Arnside Knott, a wooded limestone hill reaching over 500 feet, and as would be expected an excellent viewpoint. All of interest in the village itself is spread along the front, in the shape of two hotels and an assortment of shops. The tiny pier was savagely ripped apart by storms in the winter of 1982/83, but has now been restored to first-class condition by virtue of a £25,000 fund raised mainly by the efforts of local residents. From the pier take a long look across the bay: far into the distance beyond many intervening hills and valleys is journey's end.

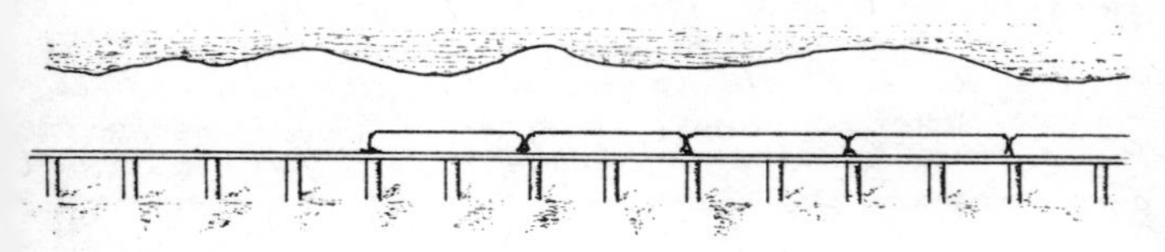

Route

The Furness Way commences on the front at Arnside. An ideal starting point is the pier, which although tiny may be recognised instantly by its surround of weary Westmorland Wayfarers sighing with relief and muttering 'never again'. They don't really mean that of course, for who knows, maybe one of them is going to keep himself active by setting out on the Furness Way tomorrow.

So, without further ado let's get off. From the pier turn right along the front (i.e. with the Bay on your right) and when the main road (Silverdale Road) climbs away from the front follow it up through the village. After levelling out the main road swings right by the Catholic church and the telephone exchange: here leave it by going straight ahead along Briery Bank to descend to a T-junction with Black Dyke Road.

Cross straight over this road and escape down a track opposite to reach the railway line, which is flanked by wicket gates. After crossing head straight across the field on a reasonable path which leads to a small footbridge over a murky drain. It continues across Arnside Moss to a similar situation at the end of the next field. A very large field is then crossed to a fence at the far end, from where a small field leads to a stile into a narrow lane.

The gapstile straight across will cause agony to any chunky fellow-walkers; from it head across the field through some small limestone outcrops towards a gate at the far end. Then however, ignore the gate in favour of a gapstile in the wall on the right. Turn left for a few yards to another gapstile by a gate. Pass through it and go forward to join a farm-track which is followed to the far end of the field. Just ahead stands Hazelslack's pele tower, which is reached by turning right along the lane after leaving the field.

Enter the farmyard at Hazelslack, and after a look at the old tower take a stile just to the right of the farmhouse to enter a field. Head for the far side to locate a well-hidden stile 25 yards to the right of a telegraph pole. It admits to another narrow lane.

ARNSIDE to HAZELSLACK

On the approach to Hazelslack the route coincides with that of the Westmorland Way. This acquaintance lasts only a few minutes

Kent Estuary
GRANGE
(B.R.)
MILNTHORPE B5282
Station
B5282
pier
THE START
Arnside
R.C. Church
telephone exchange
YH
200
SILVERDALE
SILVERDALE YEALAND
CARNFORTH (B.R.)
Arnside Moss
ARNSIDE (lane)
STORTH SANDSIDE
Hazelslack
Tower
19

Hazelslack Tower stands in the corner of a farmyard but despite its ruinous state and acquisition of foliage, still looks impressive. Like many others in the vicinity it was built in the late 14th century to afford protection from the marauding Scots who were prone to dropping by.

Route

Leave the lane by a stile straight ahead and follow a wall on the right. When it swings away aim straight ahead to an interesting stile, fronted with stone steps, in the wall corner. Navigation now eases for a good while: from the stile simply follow the wall on the left to eventually reach the far end, where the wall turns right. Follow it to a gate into the woods, from where a path climbs between the trees to a stile by a gate. Once back into daylight follow the wall on the left again, through a field surrounded completely by woodland. A stile at the far end deposits us onto a lane.

Turn right along this byway which again is enclosed by trees. This little area inland from Arnside is particularly well-endowed with public footpaths, but ignore several that head off into the trees, until a cart-track on the left signals the end of our wooded captivity. Abandon the lane in favour of the track, and it will lead unerringly to the hamlet of Haverbrack. Here it receives a layer of tarmac before bending to the right to leave Haverbrack at a minor T-junction. Here opt for a gapstile in the wall directly ahead, to enter the grounds of Dallam Tower.

Set off down the field to a kissing-gate by a large iron gate onto the public road through the park, and straight across to similar gates opposite. Bear left now, over the undulating terrain of the deer park: the house itself soon appears over to the left, and continues to hold the attention until a small stone bridge appears ahead. The River Bela provides a splendid foreground to the final view of Dallam Tower. Cross the bridge to emerge right back into the twentieth century with a jolt.

bridge over the Bela, Dallam Park

HAZELSLACK to the RIVER BELA

Dallam Tower began life as a pele tower, but since the early 18th century has been a stately mansion. Our route crosses the pleasant parkland directly in front of the house, and this being a deer park look out for these creatures which I have always been fortunate enough to see here. The River Bela flows gracefully through the park, less than a mile before its absorption into the Kent.

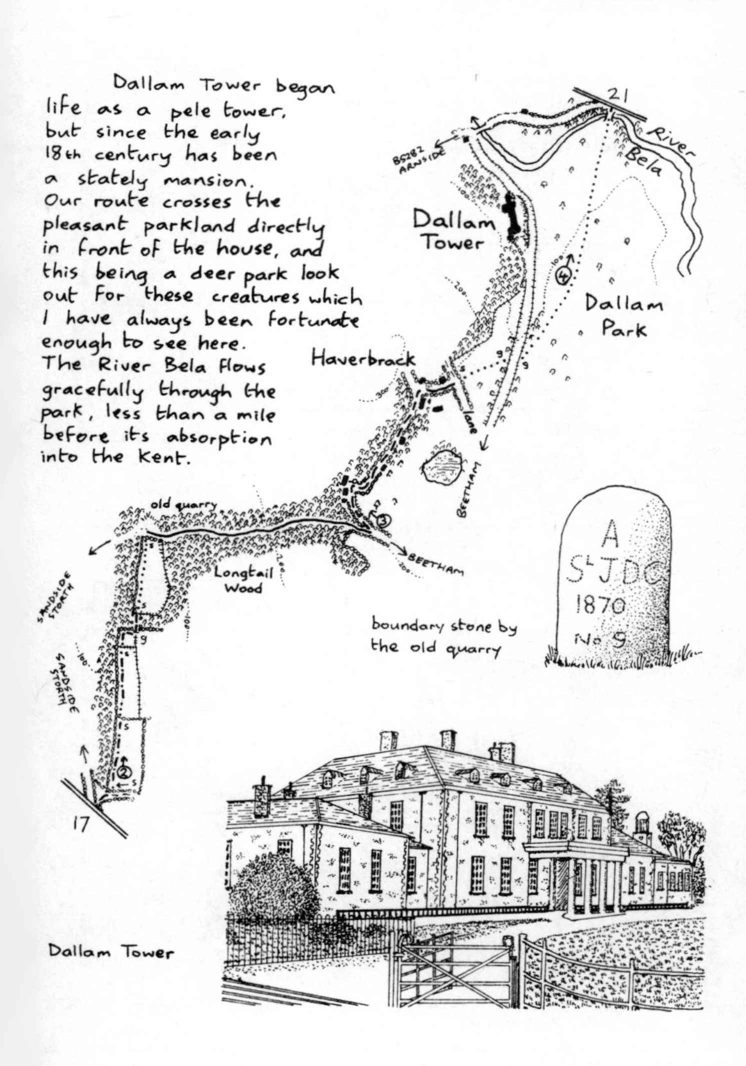

boundary stone by the old quarry

Dallam Tower

Although the centre of Milnthorpe is not visited it lies only two minutes off-route. Astride the busy A6, this typical grey-stone Westmorland village is a lively focal-point of local life. Just aside from this long-used highway is the market square adjoining the parish church, which dates from 1837 and is dedicated to St. Thomas. A most attractive modern Catholic church is hidden behind nearby houses.

8th century Anglian cross in Heversham church porch

Heversham has little in common with Milnthorpe, being smaller and much quieter with the main road long having avoided the village. It takes a parallel course to the west, for a mile along which Heversham clings to it's old road with little depth. At the 'centre' stand the church, post office and just down on the main road, the inn. The imposing church of St. Peter dates from 1601 and occupies a historically important site. The famous grammar school was founded a dozen years after the church was erected.

Heversham village

The RIVER BELA to LEVENS BRIDGE

Route

The bridge over the Bela leads onto the B5282 Milnthorpe to Arnside road on its way out of Milnthorpe. Turn right along it for a few yards only; just after the second house on the left cross the road and head past the house and up a track. As it approaches a farmyard leave it in favour of a more inviting green track to the right, enclosed by walls. It heads gradually uphill, but when it drops to the right take a gapstile into the right-hand of the two fields ahead. Go up by a hedge to the top and from the gate head over to the rear of the last house on the right. From a stile in the wall there, drop down to the right to emerge onto the A6.

Turn left along this busy highway which happily possesses a footpath. On reaching Heversham, turn right to tramp the length of the village on a much quieter lane.

After a mile the A6 is rejoined, but only for a short distance to Levens Bridge.

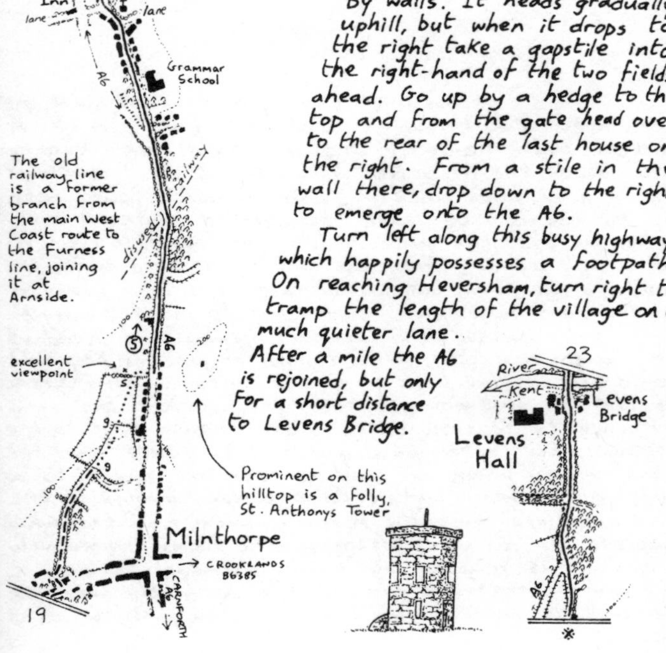

Levens Hall, the north front

Route

Cross over Levens Bridge and leave the road immediately through a small gate on the right. A sketchy path heads off through Levens Park, keeping well above the River Kent. This pleasant stroll continues for a good while until a sign deflects our path up to the left to leave the deer in peace. A stile takes us over the wall, which is then followed to the right to a wall corner. From the stile there, head across the field to the farm buildings of Park Head, from where a winding lane is followed to the left to join the busy A6.

Cross this dual-carriageway and head up the lane opposite; at a triangular junction keep right to arrive in front of a row of cottages, with the rear of the inn just down to the right, outside the main entrance to Sizergh Castle. Take the track up to the cottages, but after passing through a gate leave the track which swings left and go straight ahead to a stile in the fence corner. Climb steeply alongside the wall until level ground is reached. Turn right, through a gapstile by a gate: Sizergh Castle looms impressively ahead. It is reached by heading straight towards it, the wall on the right keeping company all the way. The car park is entered via two intervening stiles.

LEVENS BRIDGE to SIZERGH CASTLE

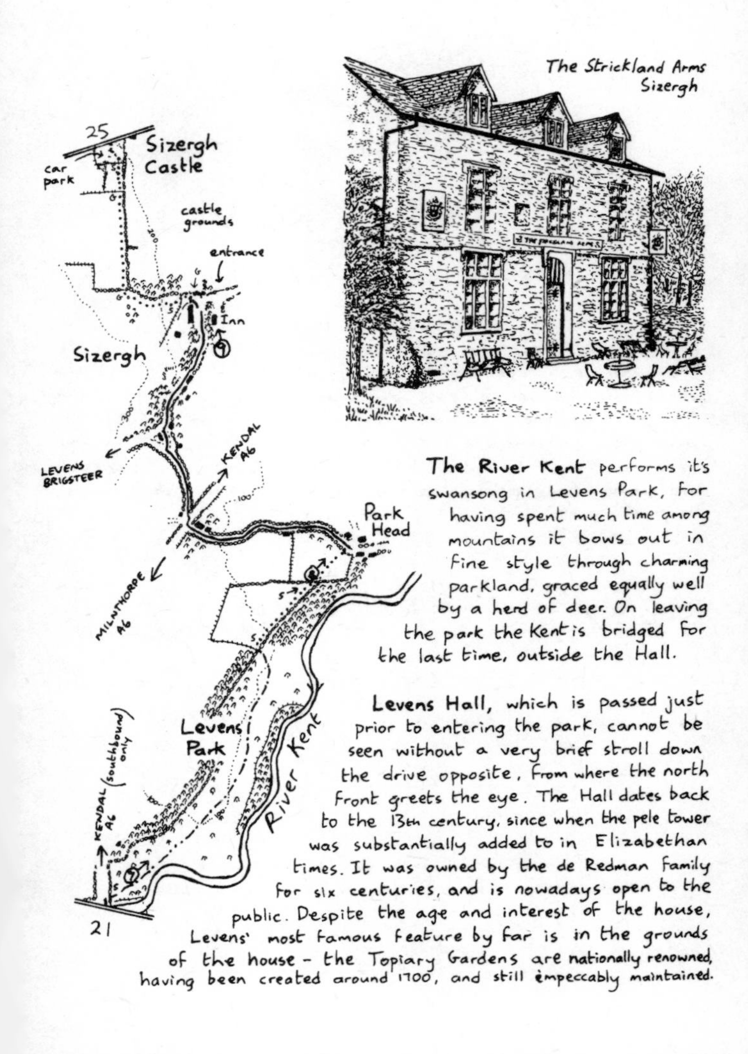

The Strickland Arms Sizergh

The River Kent performs it's swansong in Levens Park, for having spent much time among mountains it bows out in fine style through charming parkland, graced equally well by a herd of deer. On leaving the park the Kent is bridged for the last time, outside the Hall.

Levens Hall, which is passed just prior to entering the park, cannot be seen without a very brief stroll down the drive opposite, from where the north front greets the eye. The Hall dates back to the 13th century, since when the pele tower was substantially added to in Elizabethan times. It was owned by the de Redman family for six centuries, and is nowadays open to the public. Despite the age and interest of the house, Levens' most famous feature by far is in the grounds of the house - the Topiary Gardens are nationally renowned, having been created around 1700, and still impeccably maintained.

Sizergh Castle: the pele tower and east front

Sizergh Castle is a grand old house, probably the finest in old Westmorland. The oldest part is the ubiquitous pele tower, much added to in Elizabethan times: the house contains an impressive array of treasures. Sizergh has been occupied by the Strickland Family for more than an amazing 700 years, and is now also in the safe care of the National Trust. As our path crosses its car park, some aspects can be appreciated from close quarters.

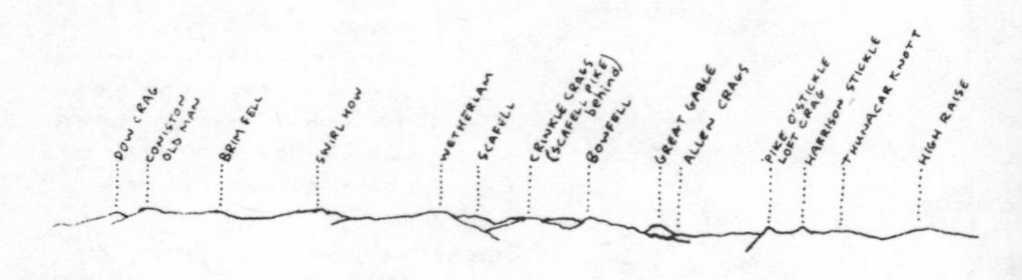

The distant central lakeland fells from Helsington Church

The wonderfully situated seat by the track outside Helsington Church bears the following words:-

'In memory of Robert Wilkinson,
who tended the gardens of
Sizergh Castle for 50 years
1896 — 1946'

SIZERGH CASTLE to BRIGSTEER

Route

Head straight across the car park to a gate in the wall opposite. It admits to an enclosed track which is followed up to the left till it emerges into a large tract of rough pasture. Remain on the path for a short distance only, to break off to climb to the right of a prominent tightly-packed copse, just past which another path is joined to continue a gradual climb with ever-improving views - the Castle itself looking impressive in retrospect. The path runs along the crest of the hill to come to a gate. From it head left along a farm road to arrive at the superbly-sited Helsington Church.

After a pleasant break, strike off the track in a north-westerly direction for Brigsteer. This diagonal descent leads to a rickety stile in a fence, to enter the woods on a good path which slopes down to join an even better one. Turn right along this broad trail to emerge onto a lane, then follow it to the left to drop down into Brigsteer village.

27 Brigsteer
KENDAL
LEVENS
11
Helsington Church
Holeslack Height
10
Sizergh Castle
23

Holeslack is the name of the farm shown. This name is just the author's idea, to mark another good viewpoint.

The lonely church of St. John, Helsington, marks the highest point reached on this opening day - it can safely be said therefore that it's the nearest we'll come to God today. Built in 1726 though much restored, it's surround of trees afford much-needed protection from the elements, the rough-cast exterior also serving this purpose. Though Helsington is the parish, the only village therein is Brigsteer.

The approach to Brigsteer

The Way only skirts the village of Brigsteer, but enough is seen to appreciate what an attractive place it is, with a large number of whitewashed cottages huddled in a somewhat haphazard fashion. In a near-idyllic setting, Brigsteer shelters under the steeply-rising slopes of Scout Scar, whilst looking west across the lush Lyth Valley.

Crosthwaite has little in common with Brigsteer, for it is a tiny community stretching over a mile along a minor lane, which carries a bus service connecting with Kendal and Bowness. Comprising mainly of scattered farms, the centre can be said to be the grouping of the two main buildings, church and inn: it is still referred to as Churchtown. The solidly-built church of St. Mary is but a century old.

Crosthwaite Church

BRIGSTEER to CROSTHWAITE

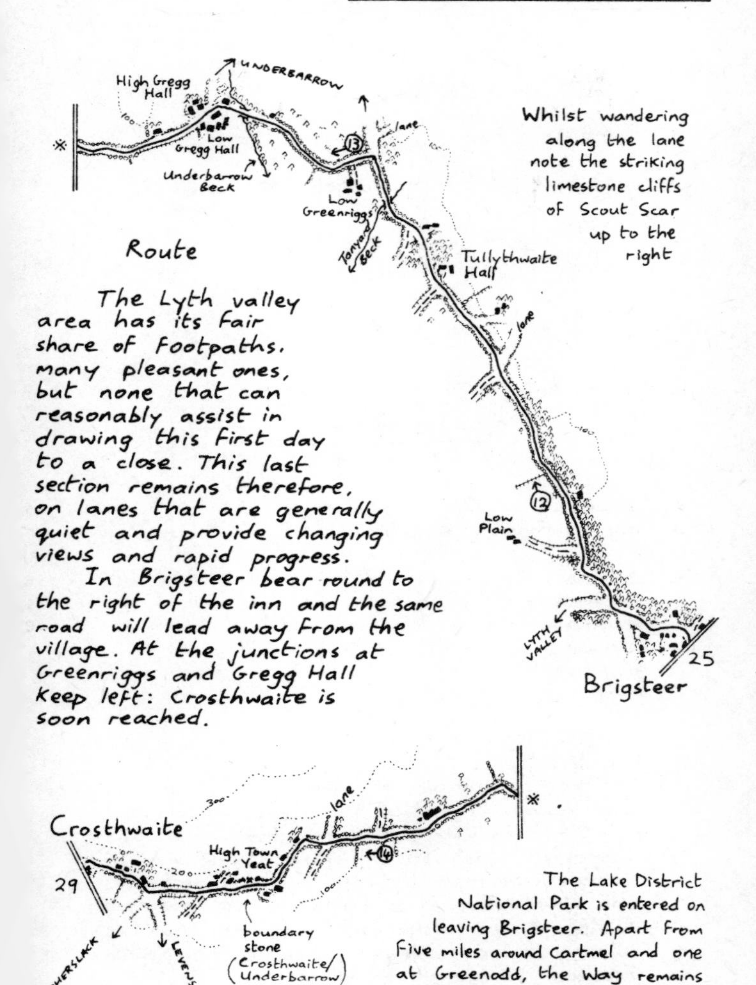

Whilst wandering along the lane note the striking limestone cliffs of Scout Scar up to the right

Route

The Lyth valley area has its fair share of footpaths, many pleasant ones, but none that can reasonably assist in drawing this first day to a close. This last section remains therefore, on lanes that are generally quiet and provide changing views and rapid progress.

In Brigsteer bear round to the right of the inn and the same road will lead away from the village. At the junctions at Greenriggs and Gregg Hall keep left: Crosthwaite is soon reached.

The Lake District National Park is entered on leaving Brigsteer. Apart from five miles around Cartmel and one at Greenodd, the Way remains within its bounds to the very end.

DAY TWO — CROSTHWAITE TO CARTMEL

Distance - 13 miles

Going - easy

Highest point - Hampsfell, 727 feet

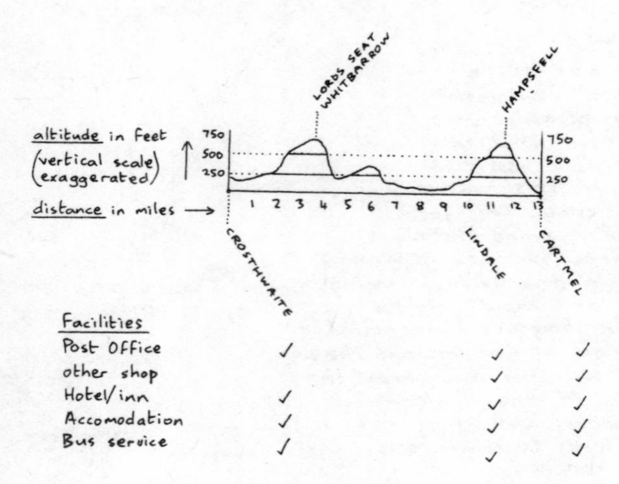

Facilities	Crosthwaite	Lindale	Cartmel
Post Office	✓	✓	✓
other shop		✓	✓
Hotel/inn	✓	✓	✓
Accomodation	✓	✓	✓
Bus service	✓	✓	✓

This is very much a day of ups and downs. The two high spots of the day are the popular fells of Whitbarrow and Hampsfell, which both display a profusion of limestone outcrops. Between these breezy heights the Way takes in a corner of the scattered settlement of Witherslack and the charming Winster valley, along with corners of Newton Fell and Lindale village. All of these relatively minor heights are excellent viewpoints

CROSTHWAITE to FELL EDGE

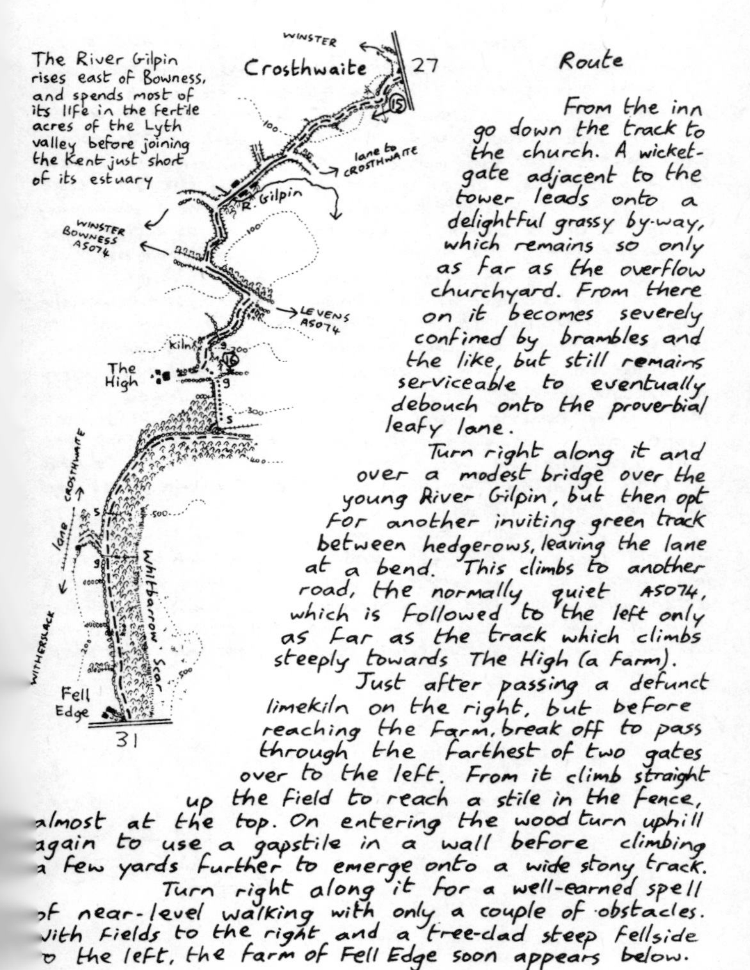

The River Gilpin rises east of Bowness, and spends most of its life in the fertile acres of the Lyth valley before joining the Kent just short of its estuary

Route

From the inn go down the track to the church. A wicket-gate adjacent to the tower leads onto a delightful grassy by-way, which remains so only as far as the overflow churchyard. From there on it becomes severely confined by brambles and the like, but still remains serviceable to eventually debouch onto the proverbial leafy lane.

Turn right along it and over a modest bridge over the young River Gilpin, but then opt for another inviting green track between hedgerows, leaving the lane at a bend. This climbs to another road, the normally quiet A5074, which is followed to the left only as far as the track which climbs steeply towards The High (a farm).

Just after passing a defunct limekiln on the right, but before reaching the farm, break off to pass through the farthest of two gates over to the left. From it climb straight up the field to reach a stile in the fence, almost at the top. On entering the wood turn uphill again to use a gapstile in a wall before climbing a few yards further to emerge onto a wide stony track.

Turn right along it for a well-earned spell of near-level walking with only a couple of obstacles. With fields to the right and a tree-clad steep fellside to the left, the farm of Fell Edge soon appears below.

Route

Shortly after passing above Fell Edge farm the path forsakes its level trod and heads away up into the trees, climbing steeply to soon rise out of the trees then passes through a pronounced gap in the limestone scar. A superb retrospective view makes the puffing and panting worthwhile. Now the gradient has eased, head away from the Scar edge to cross a stile in the parallel wall behind: accompany it till it bends away to the right. The objective now is Lords Seat, the highest point of Whitbarrow.

From the wall-corner bear slightly left up the very gradual slope, aiming for a conspicuously large boulder amidst the outcrops. On arrival it transpires there are two boulders, not one. From here continue in the same direction to reach a large cairn. A natural-looking ditch can then be followed to the left: after passing round an extensive rash of stones topped by a cairn, go straight on to arrive at the wall crossing the fell. Follow it to the left to find a stile bearing the sign of the Cumbria Trust for Nature Conservation.

A good path leads away from it through a thin surround of trees, and after a while a long low limestone scar deflects the path away from the attendant wall. The large cairn atop Lords Seat has been in view for some time, and the top is attained by following the path that climbs to it from the scar.

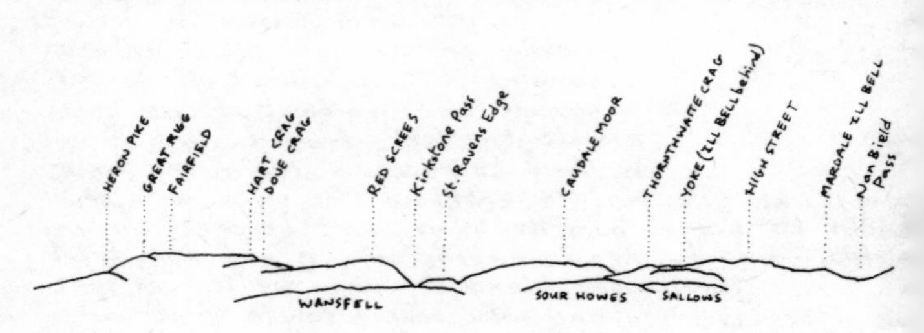

The eastern fells of Lakeland from Lords Seat

FELL EDGE to LORDS SEAT

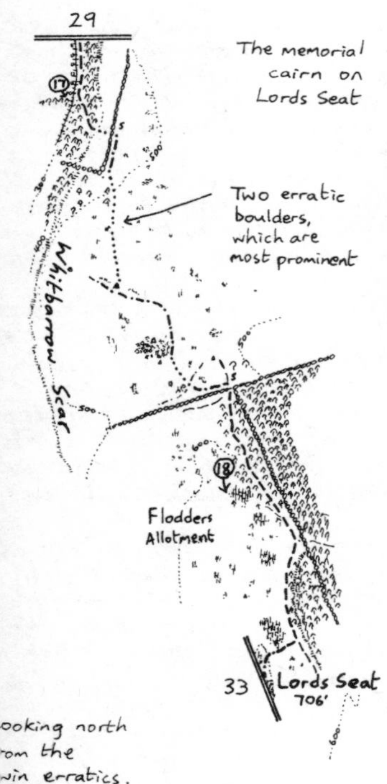

ooking north
rom the
win erratics.

The memorial cairn on Lords Seat

Whitbarrow is an immense plateau-like upland covering many square miles between the Lyth and Winster valleys. It is a major landmark in the South Westmorland area, being recognisable from all directions. The main feature is the 4½-mile-long scar along the western and southern edges of the Fell.

If the sun shines here then the brilliant white of limestone is most impressive, from the steep Scar to the profuse pavements and rocks scattered across the plateau. The summit, named Lords Seat, is surmounted by a most substantial cairn, built to commemorate the late Canon Hervey, a founder of the Lake District (now Cumbria) Naturalists Trust. This highest part is now a Nature Reserve

Route

From the cairn on Lords Seat head west to another soundly-built cairn, and continue in that direction on an excellent cairned path between an assortment of outcrops (both plant and rock). On reaching the grassy edge of the fell ensure the brakes are firmly applied as a descent from here would be rather a little too rapid. Turn left along the edge of the fell, still on terrain 'par excellence', until the path drops a little to leave the top via a gap in the wall on the right, being marked again on the opposite side by a Naturalists Trust sign.

A steep descent through the trees ensues then followed by a gentle stroll to reach a gate, preceded by a magnificently-situated football pitch. From the gate head across a field; a notice-board by the gate at the far end serves as a reminder to pause and look back at the impressive cliffs of Chapel Head Scar. From the gate a short track leads up onto a lane, with Witherslack Hall just visible up to the right.

Turn right along the lane only as far as Witherslack Hall Farm, and where the lane bends right head up a rough track to the left. On emerging from walled enclosure head diagonally across the field to a gate. Continue, still on a good track, with a wall on the left. When the wall swings away the track fades: bear half-right to pick up a tractor-track which leads to a gate in the wall opposite.

A good path now leads through delightful woodland. After a while it descends a little steeply, and when the slope curtails watch for a path breaking off to the right. It drops in a zig-zag fashion onto a quiet lane, with Witherslack Church just across to the right.

Looking back to Chapel Head Scar, on leaving Park Wood

LORDS SEAT to WITHERSLACK CHURCH

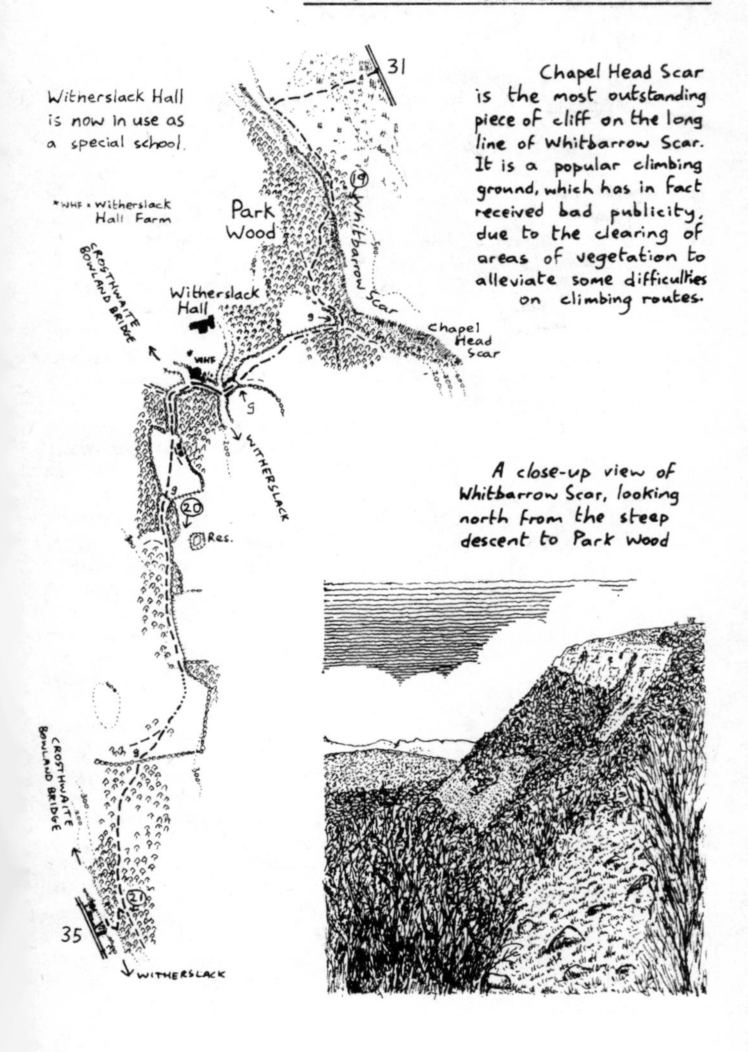

Witherslack Hall is now in use as a special school.

*WHF = Witherslack Hall Farm

Chapel Head Scar is the most outstanding piece of cliff on the long line of Whitbarrow Scar. It is a popular climbing ground, which has in fact received bad publicity, due to the clearing of areas of vegetation to alleviate some difficulties on climbing routes.

A close-up view of Whitbarrow Scar, looking north from the steep descent to Park Wood

Route

Leave Witherslack Church by means of an enclosed path (signposted to Halecat) behind the former vicarage at the other side of the green. Passing by a natural rock garden the path turns right into woodland and soon emerges onto a lane.

Cross straight over and head off on a track behind a couple of houses, only to leave it there by a path forking right through the trees to reach a stile in a fence. From it the path continues between trees before entering an open field to aim for a gate on the left. Do not use the gate but follow the wall to the right to pick up a clearer path which descends to the right through more trees. From a stile in the wall at the bottom, head round to the right of the buildings. A gate admits to the short drive that leads onto a minor lane opposite the farm of Slate Hill. A nice level stretch of the Winster valley now ensues.

The Grove

Turn left to a T-junction, then take the right fork which eventually deteriorates into a rough track. Soon after that it forks: turn right, through a gate into Nichols Wood. A good path leads to Nichols Wood Farm, continuing past it by a wall on the left to arrive at a farm bridge over the River Winster.

Cross it and follow the river downstream only as far as the first fence on the right. Then leave the river to skirt two sides of the field to a gate in the opposite corner. From it go on through three more gates. After the last one the accompanying fence on the right disappears, so head half-right to a gate in another fence. A path across rough pasture disappears by a fence corner, but go straight ahead towards a pylon at the opposite end. A gate admits to a series of pens, from where a track leads up onto a lane.

Turn right along it for a mere 100 yards, then take a large stile over the wall on the left.

WITHERSLACK CHURCH to NEWTON FELL

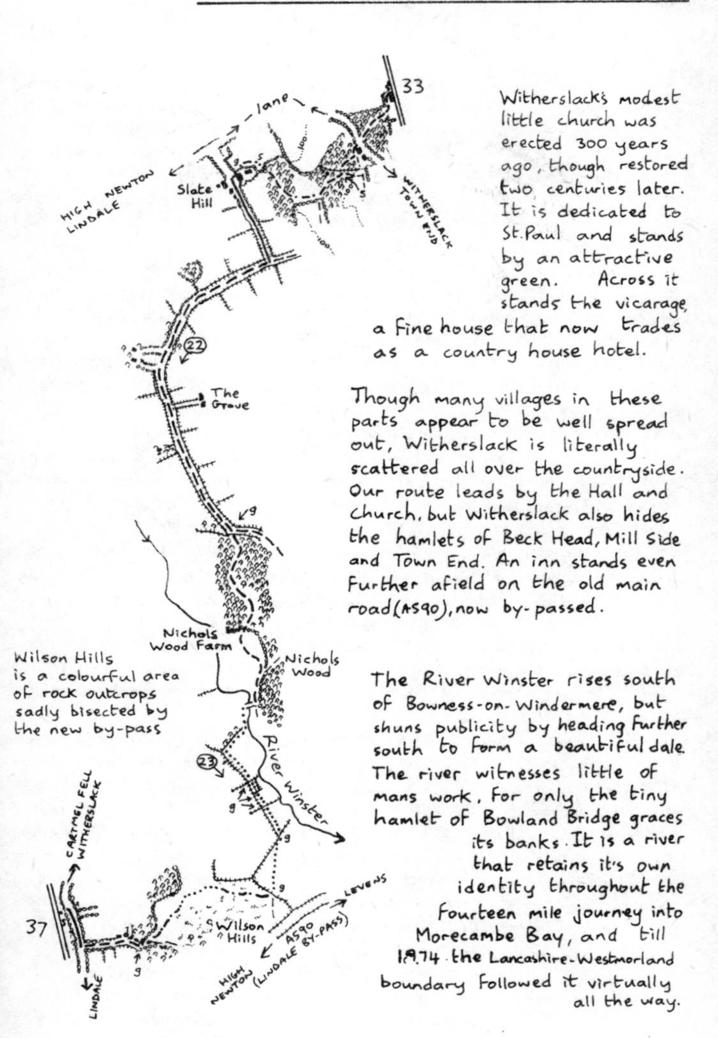

Witherslack's modest little church was erected 300 years ago, though restored two centuries later. It is dedicated to St. Paul and stands by an attractive green. Across it stands the vicarage, a fine house that now trades as a country house hotel.

Though many villages in these parts appear to be well spread out, Witherslack is literally scattered all over the countryside. Our route leads by the Hall and Church, but Witherslack also hides the hamlets of Beck Head, Mill Side and Town End. An inn stands even further afield on the old main road (A590), now by-passed.

The River Winster rises south of Bowness-on-Windermere, but shuns publicity by heading further south to form a beautiful dale. The river witnesses little of mans work, for only the tiny hamlet of Bowland Bridge graces its banks. It is a river that retains it's own identity throughout the fourteen mile journey into Morecambe Bay, and till 1974 the Lancashire-Westmorland boundary followed it virtually all the way.

Route

From the stile open fellside is immediately met. Head half-left to pick up a sketchy path rising through bramble and bracken to reach a stile over a wall to the left. Though the path becomes unclear the upward trend continues to another stile from where a superb view is obtained; this southern outpost of Newton Fell is ideal for looking back over the first two days of the Way.

The path now swings right to a gate in a short section of fence then heads away from it to yet another stile. From it descend to locate a stile built into the wall enclosing the by-pass. This dual-carriageway is crossed to a similar stile opposite. From it bear to the right of a pylon to find a stile in the wall corner. A path then descends to a lane and onto the road on the edge of Lindale village.

Turn right up this road a short distance and then left at a junction by an inn. Follow this road as far as a lane down into the village, but then head up a short cul-de-sac of modern housing on the right. At the top a rough track is joined, and almost opposite a gap-stile admits into a steeply-rising field. Follow the wall up to a wicket-gate then cross a private drive to descend through trees to a gap-stile. Head across the field to another gap-stile on the opposite slope, then climb another field to reach the tarmac drive serving Hampsfield Farm.

Leave the drive in favour of a rough track behind the large house on the left. It peters out in a field but a stile on the left rekindles a path through woods to a gap-stile. A good track now follows the wall on the left through a gate onto open fell. On reaching a stile on the left it is time to climb a zig-zag path, which itself is left, in a limestone 'amphitheatre', by going straight on to a stile in the rising wall. A right turn leads past the wall-corner to Hampsfell Hospice.

new stile, new road: Lindale by-pass from Newton Fell

NEWTON FELL to HAMPSFELL

Newton Fell runs further north for several miles: but our route accompanies it's southerly fall to Lindale. Once happily connected with the village, it is now severed by the huge sweep of the by-pass.

Like any other village similarly freed, Lindale has fallen back into more peaceful times since the heavy traffic of the A590 left it's streets. However, long before busy roads hit the headlines a local man was making his name in other areas of transport. John Wilkinson, dubbed the 'ironmaster' created the worlds first iron bridge and also experimented with iron ships. He died in 1808, and an obelisk in the village recalls his achievements.

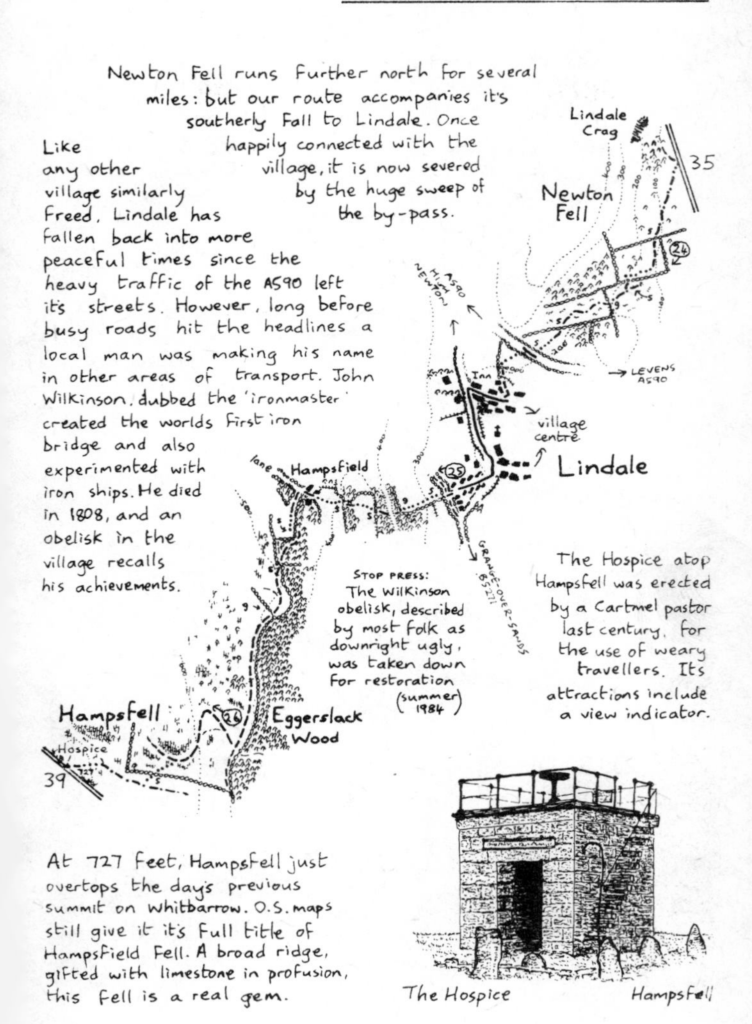

STOP PRESS: The Wilkinson obelisk, described by most folk as downright ugly, was taken down for restoration (summer 1984)

The Hospice atop Hampsfell was erected by a Cartmel pastor last century, for the use of weary travellers. Its attractions include a view indicator.

At 727 feet, Hampsfell just overtops the day's previous summit on Whitbarrow. O.S. maps still give it it's full title of Hampsfield Fell. A broad ridge, gifted with limestone in profusion, this fell is a real gem.

The Hospice Hampsfell

Cartmel may be only a small village but has more character than most. It has a unique independence, owed partly to it's lively past and also to it's geographical location. Formerly in Lancashire but not in Furness; now part of Cumbria, the all-embracing county.

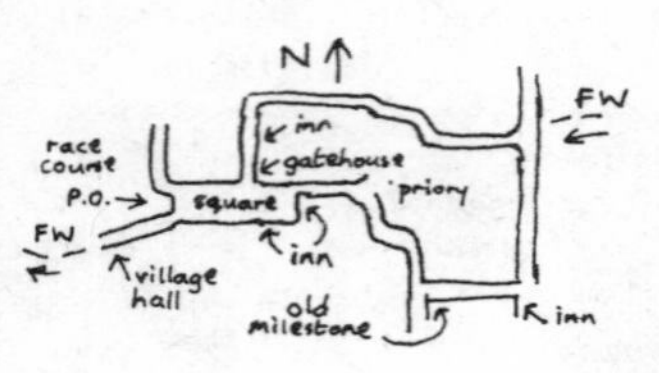

Apart from the famous Priory, other interest includes the racecourse – surely in the most charming setting of any – and the 14th century gatehouse, fortified to defend the Priory. The gatehouse still bridges the road into the square, and is open to inspection courtesy of the National Trust.

The Priory Church of St. Mary and St. Michael was founded in 1188 for Augustinian Canons, and it survived the dissolution in 1536 due to it's Parish Church status. Restored in the early 1600's, the Priory has a most sparsely decorated interior, in which lies much of it's charm. Having said this, the choir stalls and the oak screen are truly magnificent. Also of interest is the well-preserved Harrington tomb, over 600 years old.

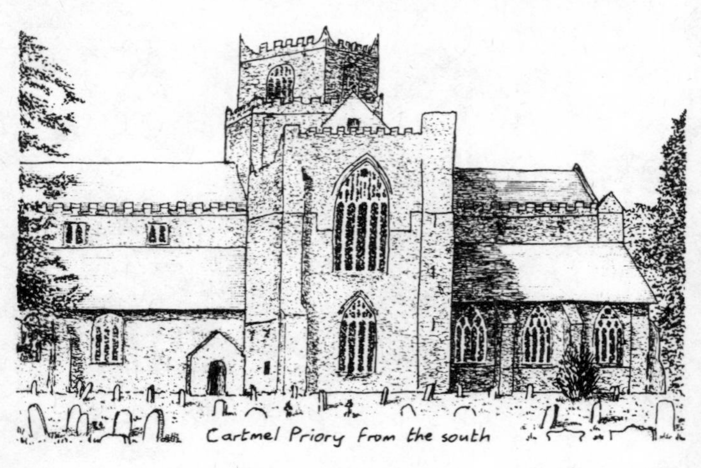

Cartmel Priory from the south

HAMPSFELL to CARTMEL

Route

From the Hospice do not consider a bee-line for Cartmel, but head due south to a well-built cairn atop a limestone ledge. Continue to a gap-stile in the wall below and on to a gap in a collapsed wall. Here leave the path by bearing a little right to begin the descent to Cartmel. A gentle gradient will lead across to the direct path down the fellside. Join it to drop rather more steeply to a gate, which signals the end of the open fell. Follow the wall on the right to another gate at the far end. Now aim diagonally across the field to the sprawl of buildings at Pit Farm.

On reaching the farm do not enter its confines but go round past the right-hand barn to locate a stile by a gate. Follow the fence across the rise of the field, Cartmel re-appearing now only minutes away. From a gate at the far end a short snicket debouches onto a lane on the edge of the village.

Turn left and then sharp right on Priest Lane to arrive at a gate into the churchyard. Use it and skirt two sides of the Priory to leave by the main gateway. Turn right for a matter of yards along the main street, which then opens out into the village square.

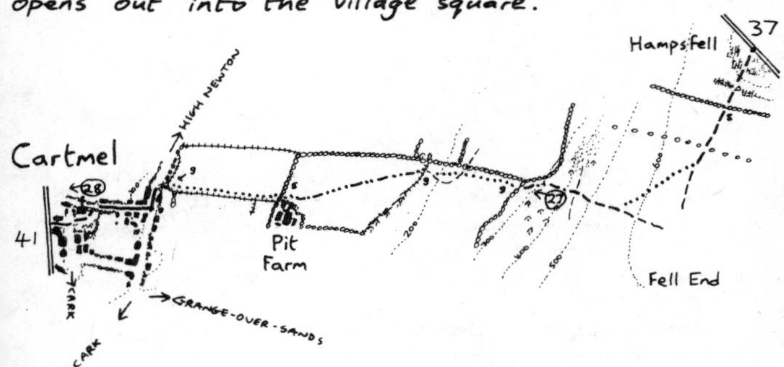

DAY THREE — CARTMEL TO LOWICK

Distance - 12½ miles

Going - easy

Highest point - Bigland Height, 610 feet

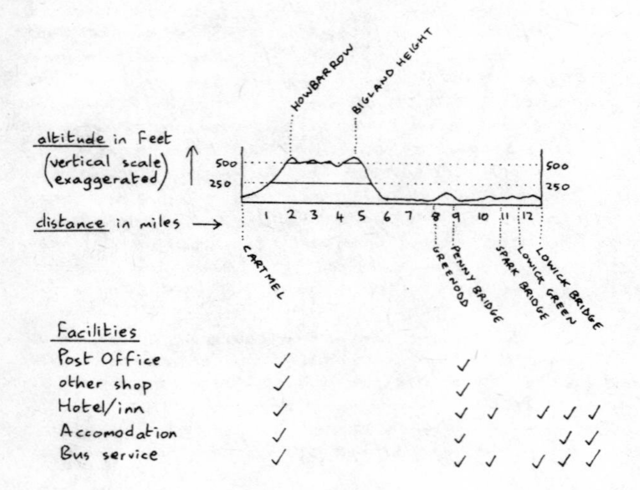

Facilities

	Cartmel	Greenodd	Penny Bridge	Spark Bridge	Lowick Green	Lowick Bridge
Post Office	✓	✓				
other shop	✓	✓				
Hotel/inn	✓	✓	✓	✓	✓	✓
Accomodation	✓	✓			✓	✓
Bus service	✓	✓	✓	✓	✓	✓

The walk from Cartmel to Lowick consists of two distinct halves. Firstly a broad undulating ridge high above the Leven estuary is traversed from Howbarrow to Bigland Tarn, then a descent to valley level is followed by a complete change of environment. The River Leven is accompanied to Greenodd, from where the Way strikes inland to follow the well-wooded valley of the River Crake through several tiny villages to Lowick Green.

CARTMEL to HOWBARROW FARM

Route

From the village square take the lane to the left of the post office to enter the racecourse. After crossing the actual track bear half-right to pass the cricket pitch and cross the football pitch: an obvious gap in the fence leads across the track itself again to reach a kissing-gate into the woods.

A good path climbs initially but soon levels out, and ignoring any lesser turn-offs leave the trees by a narrow gap-stile into a field. Accompany the wall on the right to another gap-stile into a lane. This quiet lane can now be followed all the way to its demise, at the entrance to Howbarrow Farm.

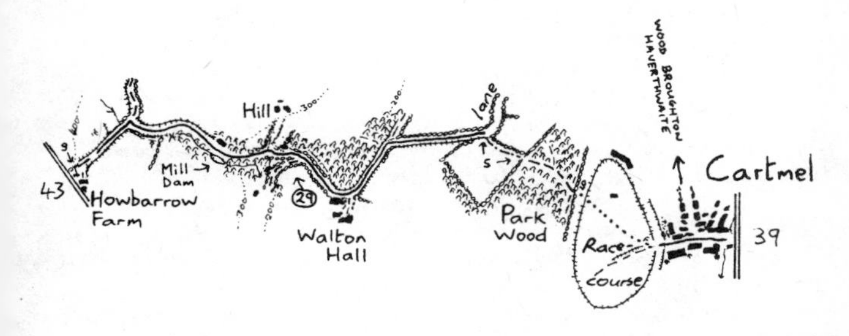

The approach to Howbarrow Farm

Route

Do not enter the farmyard but follow the track through a gate on the right to climb up past the farm buildings. At the brow of the hill not only does the Leven estuary make its first appearance but the sturdy little height of Howbarrow stands just ahead. To reach it go through the gate, where the track ends, and across the field to another gate: from it turn sharp right to climb steeply to attain the trig. point

After admiring the view from a comfortable rock, head north-east to go through a gate in the wall to join a good track heading north. On reaching a gate it becomes less clear, but improves a little after passing just to the right of the relatively large rock straight ahead. From the gate in the next cross-wall a surround of bracken adds further to the delights of this upland trek. The path bears right to join a wall which remains in close attendance until, with views across the estuary to Greenodd, a gate is reached. Use it and follow the path by the wall on the right, till it leaves it by bearing left to head northward again. The path becomes indistinct before meeting another path, then followed to the left to a gate in the wall.

Shortly after the gate the path forks: take the left one which passes between large outcrops then descends to pass between fences marking the route of the recently dug pipeline to reach a gate. Turn right along the lane but then double back along a track to the lone dwelling of Grassgarth. Pass along the left side of the house to a private-looking gate into the field behind. The wall on the right leads to a gate into High Stribers Wood.

A most pleasant path climbs through the trees accompanied throughout by a recently-erected fence. The path leaves the wood by another gate and emerges onto some more colourful upland. After a short time contouring across the hillside a track forks up to the right. This minor diversion is most worthwhile for from the top a birds-eye view of Bigland Tarn greets the eye, along with much more besides. Descend towards it and follow the path which heads left to the tarn's south-western tip.

HOWBARROW FARM to BIGLAND TARN

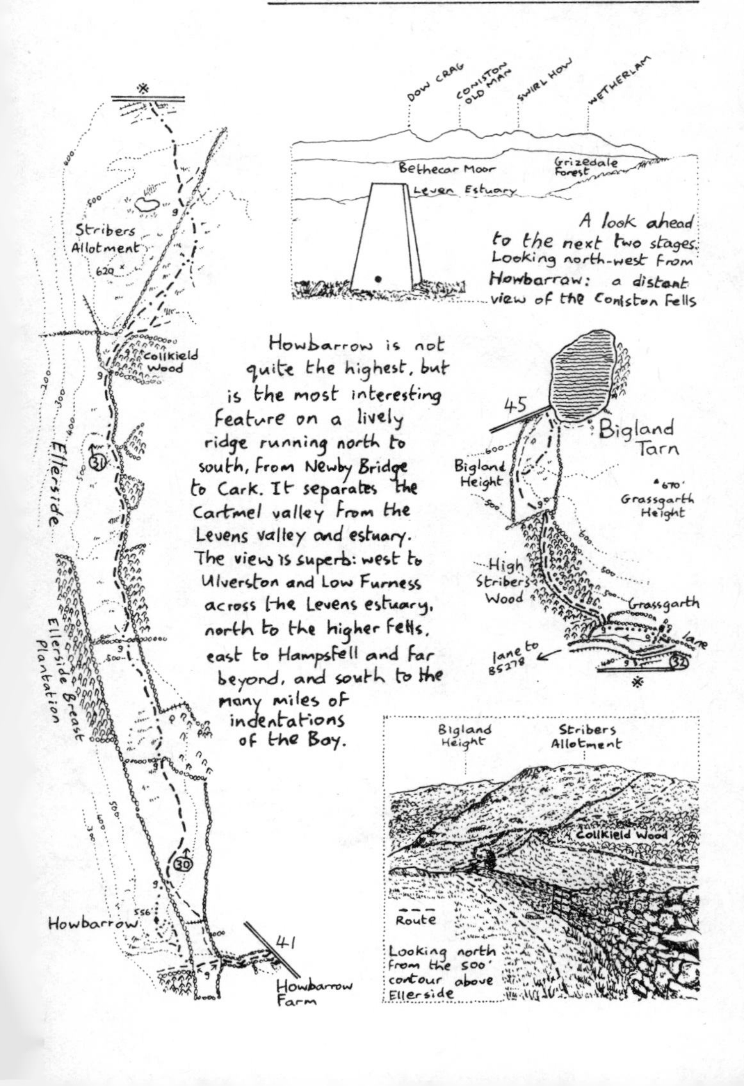

Howbarrow is not quite the highest, but is the most interesting feature on a lively ridge running north to south, from Newby Bridge to Cark. It separates the Cartmel valley from the Levens valley and estuary. The view is superb: west to Ulverston and Low Furness across the Levens estuary, north to the higher fells, east to Hampsfell and far beyond, and south to the many miles of indentations of the Bay.

BIGLAND TARN to the RIVER LEVEN

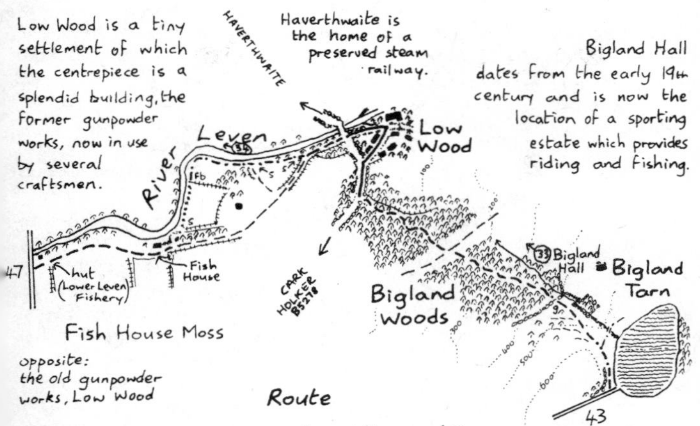

Low Wood is a tiny settlement of which the centrepiece is a splendid building, the former gunpowder works, now in use by several craftsmen.

Haverthwaite is the home of a preserved steam railway.

Bigland Hall dates from the early 19th century and is now the location of a sporting estate which provides riding and fishing.

opposite: the old gunpowder works, Low Wood

Route

On approaching the outflow from Bigland Tarn, bear left to commence a long and direct descent on an improving path, ignoring several others branching off to the left. With the beck just across to the right the path becomes steeper and soon reaches a gate to enter Bigland Wood. The only break between this gate and the valley bottom comes when a broad path is encountered: from it go straight ahead to rejoin our own path which winds and twists a little before accompanying a fence down to the road, half a mile short of Haverthwaite.

Turn right along it but then make a detour on a lane to the right to pass through the interesting old hamlet of Low Wood. A left turn after the last building leads back to the main road at Low Wood Bridge. Do not cross it but set off along the inviting track opposite. When it swings away from the river take a stile into a meadow to remain by the waterside. A stile by a gate at the far end keeps us in touch with the river, and the bank is followed closely as a tiny footbridge, another stile and some stepping stones lead to a wide gravelly track. Follow it to the right past the ruinous Fish House, with the River Leven in close proximity.

Route

The well-made track permits fast walking and the entrance to Roudsea Wood is soon reached. After a brief lesson about the Nature Reserve head off into the wood. The track remains as clear as ever, and in fact even displays a layer of tarmac for a spell. In no time at all the trees come to an end, and the track emerges from the wood with a view directly ahead to the grey dwellings of Greenodd almost on top of each other up the hillside.

The track aims straight for them, and when it turns sharply left to the isolated farm of Mearness, maintain the bee-line on a path that rises over a 'flood barrier' which rather surprisingly does not provide the anticipated view of the river. Undaunted, pass through a gateway down in front and follow the fence on the left to then climb again to a stile in a new fence. This time a lively scene lies ahead; directly in front is a long concrete footbridge, which is used to cross the Leven in rather grand style.

On reaching the busy road follow it to the left for a short distance then cross it with care to enter Greenodd at it's southernmost extremity. Turn right along the main street but then leave it by the steep lane forking up to the left.

Greenodd

The RIVER LEVEN to GREENODD

As the outflow from Windermere, Englands largest lake, the Leven is a ready-made river of substantial proportion. It's journey to form one of the main inlets of Morecambe Bay is but short. Bridged by only five roads, the final bridge is a modern footbridge, a costly structure for the right of way that disappeared when the railway viaduct was dismantled.

Greenodd is a small village guarding the entrance to the Crake valley, standing watch at the confluence with the Leven, itself about to enter the Bay. The place had a lively past, having once been a thriving little port with it's own railway station, and until the recent by-pass, astride the main A590. Instead, it's main street has gone to the other extreme and become a cul-de-sac.

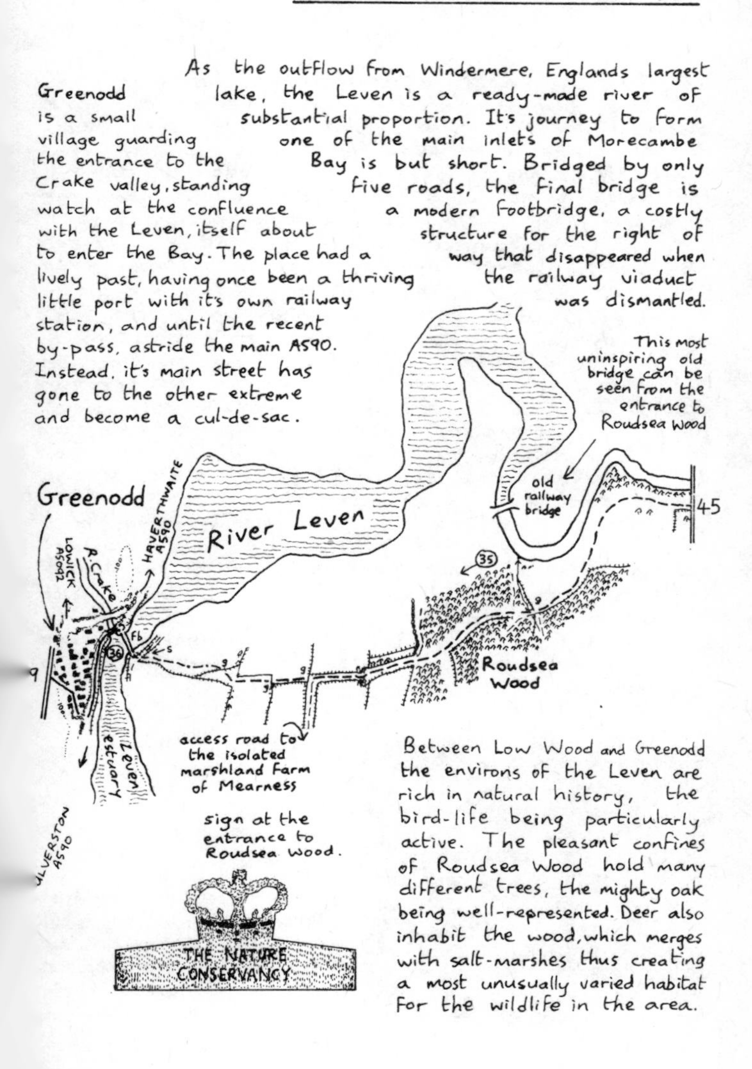

Between Low Wood and Greenodd the environs of the Leven are rich in natural history, the bird-life being particularly active. The pleasant confines of Roudsea Wood hold many different trees, the mighty oak being well-represented. Deer also inhabit the wood, which merges with salt-marshes thus creating a most unusually varied habitat for the wildlife in the area.

Route

After a strenuous pull the lane levels out on reaching the school, and goes on to arrive at a T-junction from where a right turn leads down a lane lined with the houses (and inn) that constitute Penny Bridge. At the bottom of the hill the A5092 is met at a crossroads. Turn left along the main road for a 10-minute walk to a roadside farm.

Squeeze through a gapstile by a gate just opposite the farm and cross a footbridge over the River Crake to follow it downstream for a few yards only. The path then winds up to the left, past a derelict mill to the start of a long terrace of former millworkers cottages. Leave the track on this sharp bend and take a gate on the left. Contour across the field till the wall drops away then slope down to a step-stile in a fence, meeting the same again a little further along. Just down on the left is an old mill race, which is followed to the sluice-gate at the start of it's split with the river.

Here we leave the river by means of a strange old stile. From it follow the field boundary bearing half-right away from the river: At the top of the field pass through a gateway and remain with the wall on the right to reach a lane adjacent to Lane Head Farm. Turn left along the lane to descend gradually into the tidy village of Spark Bridge.

The approach to the Church of St. Mary the Virgin. This is the parish church for Spark Bridge, Penny Bridge and Greenodd, all under the jurisdiction of the parish of Egton-cum-Newland.

GREENODD to SPARK BRIDGE

Spark Bridge

Spark Bridge is a tiny village stood mainly on the west bank of the Crake. A pleasant green lies adjacent to the river, as does a surviving bobbin mill which dominates the village adding in fact a certain character to the place. A relatively important junction exists here, for lanes head away from the bridge in five directions to the nearby villages.

The River Crake was once a hive of activity, with bobbin mills spread along its banks providing the goods for the cotton industry in Lancashire early last century. Interesting evidence abounds in our short spell alongside the river. The Crake runs for only five miles from the foot of Coniston Water to the Leven estuary at Greenodd.

Penny Bridge consists of a sloping main street, a crossroads with the A5092, and once again a variety of directions in which to leave.

LOWICK BRIDGE (lane)
COLTON (lane)
51
Spark Bridge
GREENODD
BOUTH (lane)
Lane Head
LOWICK CONISTON A5092
River Crake
38
Fb
OXENPARK
BOUTH
River Crake
37
Penny Bridge
Inn
A5092
ARRAD FOOT ULVERSTON
Greenodd
47

Route

From the bridge itself head up the road towards Coniston, but soon after passing the inn take a narrow lane off to the right. This lane soon forks, and here leave it for a snicket almost straight ahead (before entering it turn to see a house renovated with a fine spinning gallery). The snicket is interrupted briefly by a yard, but then continues in excellent fashion, mostly between hedgerows with good views across the Crake. All too soon a track is joined which leads up to the left to emerge onto the A5084 at the entrance to Lowick Green. Turn right to find the large green, with the main group of houses lining the far side of it.

If the day isn't planned to end until Lowick Bridge is reached, then stay on the road, and soon after the last building on the left take a stile built into the wall. From here the map opposite takes over: use it to cross the fields to Lowick Church, free of difficulty and saving some complicated lines of text.

A lane runs in front of the church, and it should be followed down to the right for a few minutes stroll into Lowick Bridge.

The Farmers Arms, Lowick

SPARK BRIDGE to LOWICK

Lowick Parish Church was built around a century ago of distinctively local materials. Dedicated to St. Luke, it stands in a superb setting looking north to the Coniston fells. The churchyard crocus display is unforgettable.

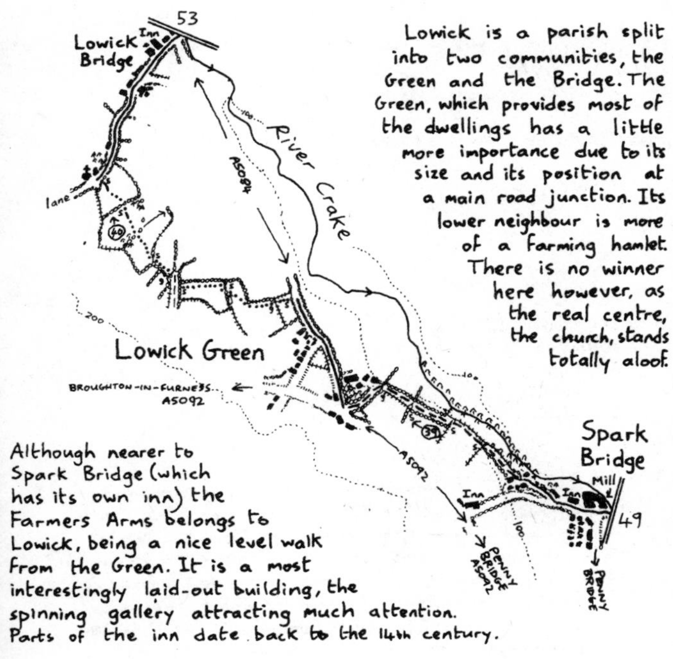

Lowick is a parish split into two communities, the Green and the Bridge. The Green, which provides most of the dwellings has a little more importance due to its size and its position at a main road junction. Its lower neighbour is more of a farming hamlet. There is no winner here however, as the real centre, the church, stands totally aloof.

Although nearer to Spark Bridge (which has its own inn) the Farmers Arms belongs to Lowick, being a nice level walk from the Green. It is a most interestingly laid-out building, the spinning gallery attracting much attention. Parts of the inn date back to the 14th century.

DAY FOUR — LOWICK TO CONISTON

Distance – 11 miles

Going – moderate

Highest point – Top O'Selside, 1091'

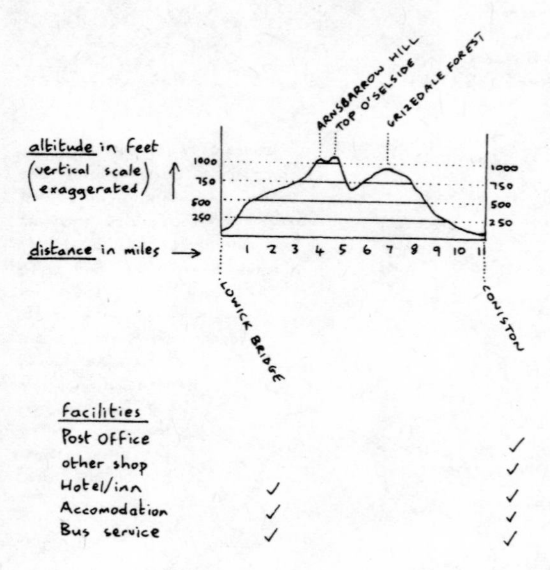

facilities	Lowick Bridge	Coniston
Post Office		✓
other shop		✓
Hotel/inn	✓	✓
Accomodation	✓	✓
Bus service	✓	✓

This fourth day is mostly an upland trek, high above the east side of the Crake valley and the entire length of Coniston Water. Hill farming environs lead to Bethecar Moor and two 1000 foot tops, then the extensive Grizedale Forest is encountered before reaching the head of the lake, and Coniston village itself. The Coniston Fells dominate the views throughout the day.

LOWICK to STOCK FARM

Route

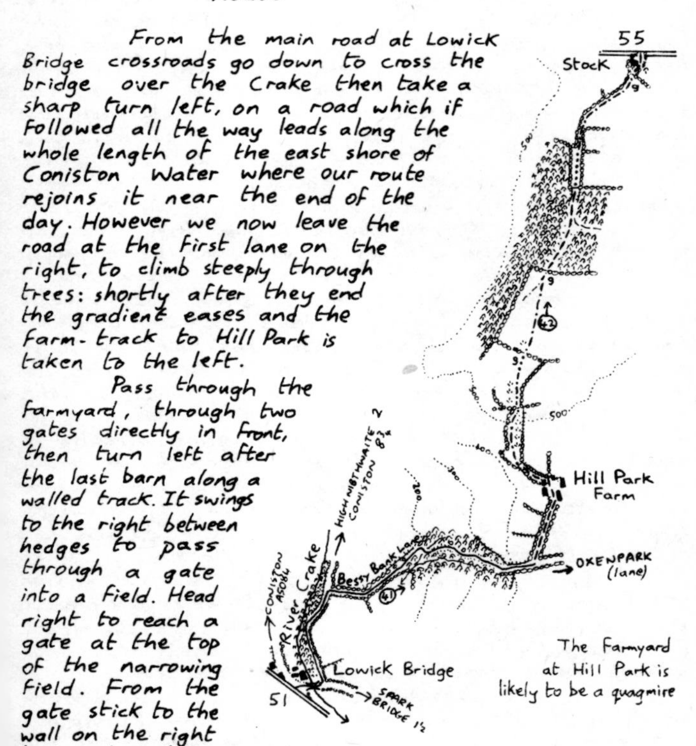

The Farmyard at Hill Park is likely to be a quagmire

From the main road at Lowick Bridge crossroads go down to cross the bridge over the Crake then take a sharp turn left, on a road which if followed all the way leads along the whole length of the east shore of Coniston Water where our route rejoins it near the end of the day. However we now leave the road at the first lane on the right, to climb steeply through trees: shortly after they end the gradient eases and the farm-track to Hill Park is taken to the left.

Pass through the farmyard, through two gates directly in front, then turn left after the last barn along a walled track. It swings to the right between hedges to pass through a gate into a field. Head right to reach a gate at the top of the narrowing field. From the gate stick to the wall on the right to avoid a little marshy area. On reaching a stile don't use it but head half-left away from the wall to reach a gate which appears ahead. From it head straight across to enter a wood via another gate.

A clear green path leads through the trees and emerges into a walled way. When the wall on the right departs, go straight on to enter the farmyard at Stock.

Route

Pass straight through the farmyard at Stock and out onto the access track: when it joins a lane turn right along it. On passing through a gate the lane degenerates into a track. Take the left branch alongside the wall, now in rough pasture. After passing through another gate the path rises round to reach Low Bethecar, a farm now used simply as a barn. Climb the slope behind on a tractor-track to pass through the right hand of two gates to follow the intake wall, once again on the left. Ten minutes further walking leads to a slight drop to meet the track from High Bethecar leaving its cultivated confines through a gate in the wall.

Turn right to follow this wide green track, which soon becomes narrower and less green. Just before it drops to cross a sluggish little stream with a 'plank' footbridge, a tiny cairn indicates the point to turn off for Arnsbarrow Hill. This top should be identified easily as it is by far the shapeliest acclivity in the vicinity. It rises from the undulating moorland to our right, with the bulk of Top O'Selside directly in front, to the left of and set further back than Arnsbarrow Hill. If the very sketchy path cannot be located or followed in full, then do not waste time searching but aim straight for the fell, bearing a little to the right to avoid marshy ground.

Once at the foot of the steepest section a path can be located on which to make the pleasant climb to the heathery top, passing en route above the only outcrop of crag on this days walk. A neat little summit cairn provides a good resting place.

On leaving, head north again on a path which soon peters out in a depression. Continue onward through the sea of heather, and before long the almost circular Arnsbarrow Tarn appears ahead. Drop down to it, preferably avoiding the environs of the outflow by bearing round to the right of the tarn.

Summit cairn, Arnsbarrow Hill

STOCK FARM to ARNSBARROW TARN

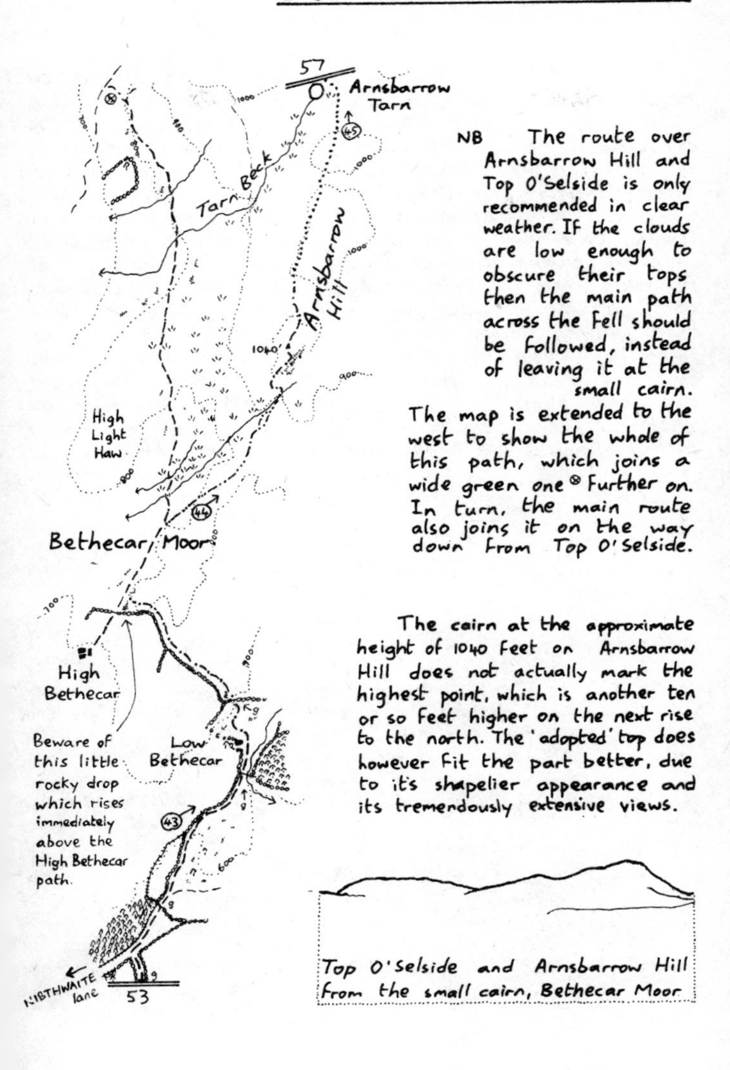

NB The route over Arnsbarrow Hill and Top O'Selside is only recommended in clear weather. If the clouds are low enough to obscure their tops then the main path across the fell should be followed, instead of leaving it at the small cairn.

The map is extended to the west to show the whole of this path, which joins a wide green one ⊗ further on. In turn, the main route also joins it on the way down from Top O'Selside.

The cairn at the approximate height of 1040 feet on Arnsbarrow Hill does not actually mark the highest point, which is another ten or so feet higher on the next rise to the north. The 'adopted' top does however fit the part better, due to it's shapelier appearance and its tremendously extensive views.

Top O'Selside and Arnsbarrow Hill from the small cairn, Bethecar Moor

Route

From Arnsbarrow Tarn swing round to head west, up the gently-rising slope that soon culminates in the cairn on Top O'Selside. It is fortunate that the climb is short, as progress is slow in the thick heather, the only sign of paths being the trods of the local sheep.

After a survey of the magnificent view leave the cairn in a north-westerly direction to descend fairly steeply to the wide green path that is mentioned in the notes on page 55; it contours the fellside about 300 feet below. Turn to the right along it, to reach a fork with the former farm of Spy Hill on the rising slope ahead. Take the left fork to descend to cross a beck, and from the gate climb between the buildings at Spy Hill to enter a field. Follow the fence on the right and pass through a gateway in the wall ahead.

continued across

The Coniston Fells from Top O'Selside

ARNSBARROW TARN to GRIZEDALE FOREST

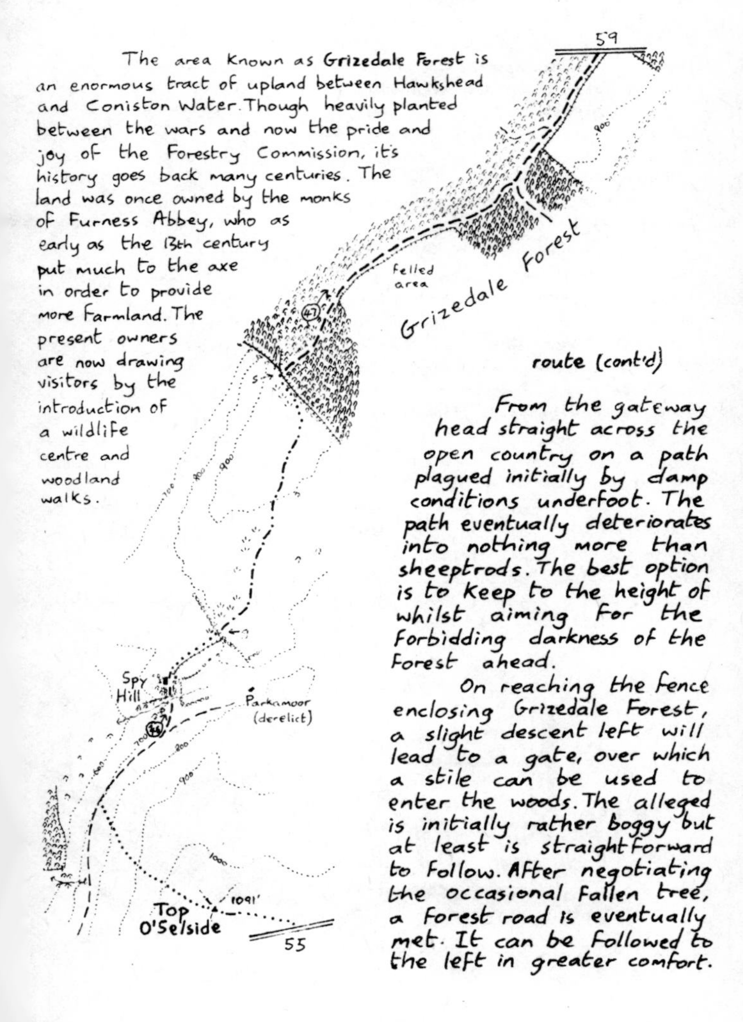

The area known as **Grizedale Forest** is an enormous tract of upland between Hawkshead and Coniston Water. Though heavily planted between the wars and now the pride and joy of the Forestry Commission, it's history goes back many centuries. The land was once owned by the monks of Furness Abbey, who as early as the 13th century put much to the axe in order to provide more farmland. The present owners are now drawing visitors by the introduction of a wildlife centre and woodland walks.

route (cont'd)

From the gateway head straight across the open country on a path plagued initially by damp conditions underfoot. The path eventually deteriorates into nothing more than sheeptrods. The best option is to keep to the height of whilst aiming for the forbidding darkness of the forest ahead.

On reaching the fence enclosing Grizedale Forest, a slight descent left will lead to a gate, over which a stile can be used to enter the woods. The alleged is initially rather boggy but at least is straightforward to follow. After negotiating the occasional fallen tree, a forest road is eventually met. It can be followed to the left in greater comfort.

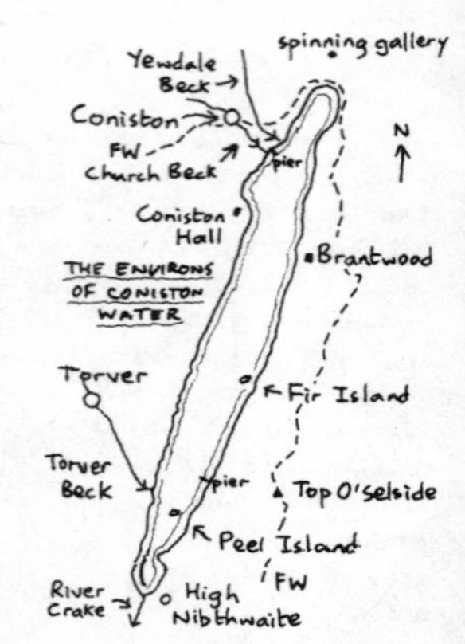

Coniston Water is the fourth largest of the English Lakes and until 1974 it was the largest in Lancashire. A typical ribbon lake, a legacy from the ice age, this five mile long sheet of water seperates the high fells of Coniston from the tamer slopes of Bethecar Moor and Grizedale Forest.

Many famous people have had strong connections with the lake. Three in chronological order are John Ruskin, who lived for many years at the splendid house of Brantwood overlooking the lake; Arthur Ransome, author of the popular children's story 'Swallows and Amazons', which was set on and around two tiny islands towards the lower end of the lake; and finally Donald Campbell, the brave world water speed record-breaker who was tragically killed whilst attempting to beat his own record on the lake in January 1967.

A most pleasing sight, only recently returned to duty on the lake is the Victorian steam yacht 'Gondola'. After almost 80 years service the boat ceased operating in 1937, then after 40 dormant years the National Trust painstakingly restored this elegant craft which resumed its former role in 1980.

The steam yacht Gondola on Coniston Water

GRIZEDALE FOREST to WATERHEAD

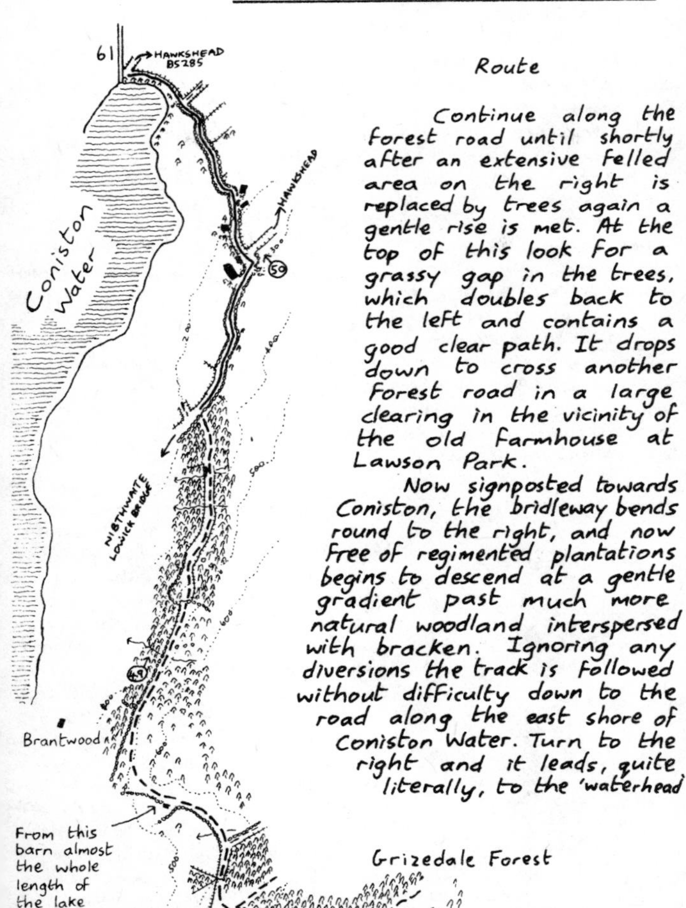

Route

Continue along the forest road until shortly after an extensive felled area on the right is replaced by trees again a gentle rise is met. At the top of this look for a grassy gap in the trees, which doubles back to the left and contains a good clear path. It drops down to cross another forest road in a large clearing in the vicinity of the old farmhouse at Lawson Park.

Now signposted towards Coniston, the bridleway bends round to the right, and now free of regimented plantations begins to descend at a gentle gradient past much more natural woodland interspersed with bracken. Ignoring any diversions the track is followed without difficulty down to the road along the east shore of Coniston Water. Turn to the right and it leads, quite literally, to the 'waterhead

Coniston is the most colourful village to be encountered on the Furness Way. It is one of Lakeland's most popular centres and in consequence the vast crowds of midsummer visitors are a heavy strain on the accomodation resources. As with all the districts larger villages, the casual visitors far outweigh the regular walkers. The attractive slate buildings shelter under the towering fells which are crowned by the Old Man of Coniston, from whose slopes much of the slate was quarried. Though the chief industry here has long been tourism, quarrying still provides employment for local people, lakeland slate being in virtual world-wide demand.

village plan, not to scale (buildings omitted)

Key
A - Parish Church
B - Ruskin cross
C - Campbell memorial
D - Ruskin Museum
E - to Coppermines YHA
F - to pier and boats

The most interesting old building hereabouts is Coniston Hall, a late 16th century manor house standing away from the village near the lakeshore. The Church of St. Andrew dates from 1819; built, naturally, of local slate, it has a most spacious interior. In the churchyard can be found with little difficulty, an enormous anglo-saxon type cross commemorating John Ruskin, who died here in 1900 after spending the last 30 years of his life at Brantwood across the lake - Coniston churchyard was his preference to Westminster Abbey. A museum was opened in the village centre soon after his death, and the big house itself is open to the public.

The Ruskin cross

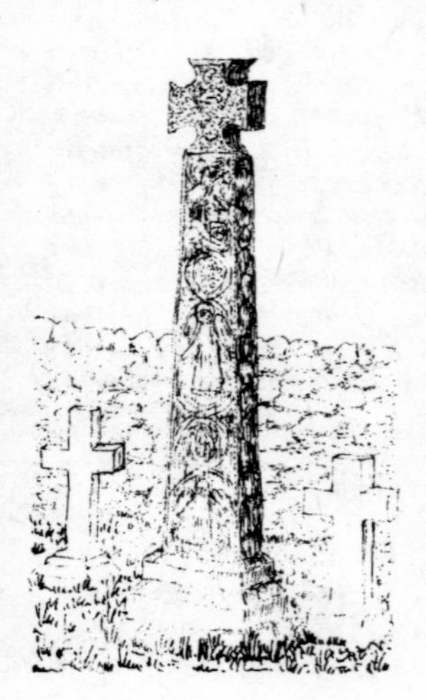

Also of local slate is the memorial to Donald Campbell, which takes the form of a T-shaped seat layout on the small green. Do not however be misled by these memorials - Coniston village is very much alive with a healthy air about it's busy streets.

WATERHEAD to CONISTON

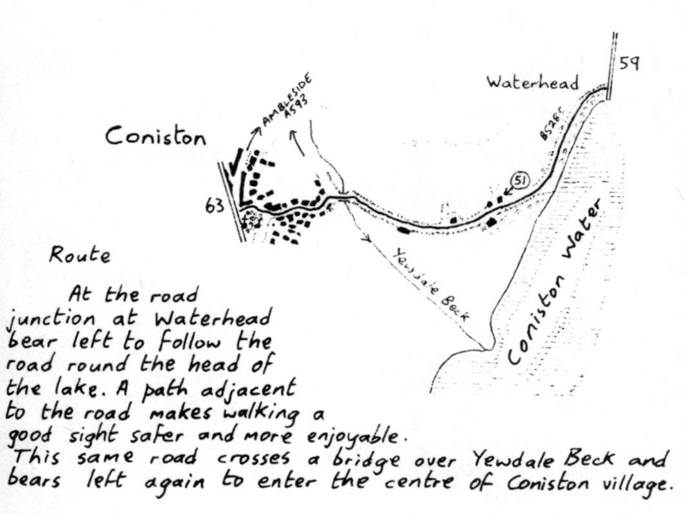

Route

At the road junction at Waterhead bear left to follow the road round the head of the lake. A path adjacent to the road makes walking a good sight safer and more enjoyable. This same road crosses a bridge over Yewdale Beck and bears left again to enter the centre of Coniston village.

Coniston village

DAY FIVE — CONISTON TO BOOT

Distance - 13 miles

Going - moderate to strenuous

Highest point - Walna Scar Pass, 1990 feet

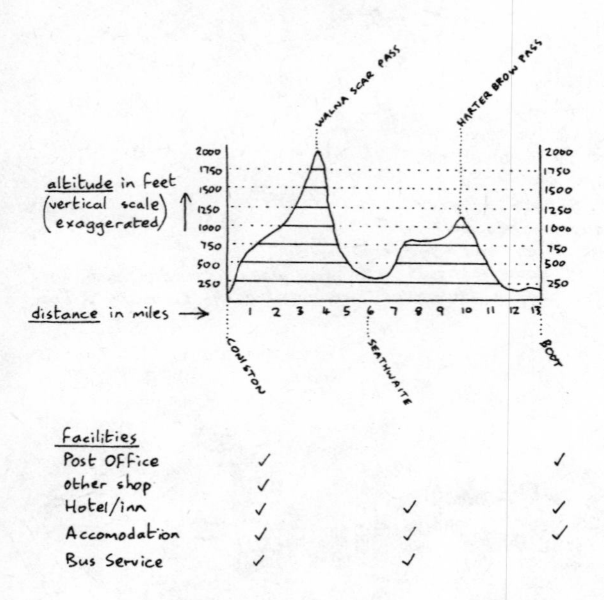

Facilities	Coniston	Seathwaite	Boot
Post Office	✓		✓
other shop	✓		
Hotel/inn	✓	✓	✓
Accomodation	✓	✓	✓
Bus Service	✓	✓	

This penultimate day requires the most effort, although gradients are, on the whole, fairly gentle. The centuries-old Walna Scar track leads to Seathwaite in the Duddon valley for a perfectly-sited midday rest. The second half of the day entails a crossing of the shoulder of Harter Fell to descend amidst glorious views into Eskdale.

CONISTON to BOO TARN

Route

To leave the village, set off from the church gate and cross the narrow road bridge over Church Beck, in the village centre. Turn right immediately, up a lane between a cafe and the beck, to pass the Sun Hotel. The lane meets another road on a bend: turn right to head up the road which at once starts to climb steeply alongside a small beck. This is the start of the Walna Scar 'road' on which we remain for the first half of the day. After a fairly relentless pull the tarmac ends at a gate. Take the main track bearing left across the open fell; almost level walking leads to the pool of Boo Tarn.

Coniston
61
300
400
500
52
600
700
TORVER A593
9
quarry road
1100
1000
900
53
65
Boo Tarn
800

The Walna Scar Road was once an important route across the hills, linking the Duddon valley with Coniston. Though some quarrying remains the horses that trod this way have been replaced by walkers, who are rewarded with excellent views of the Coniston Fells.

The rough track which leaves our path to climb the steep fellside still services a slate quarry high on the slopes of the Old Man. Just watch the wagons negotiate the zig-zags!

Boo Tarn, choked with reeds, looking to the Troutbeck fells

The Coniston Fells

Between the upper valley of the River Duddon and Coniston village rises the compact group of mountains which are popularly referred to as the Coniston Fells. Seven distinct summits rise to above 2500 feet, and all of them can be attained in a single days expedition, by virtue of the pleasant inter-connecting ridges.

By turning their backs on the Duddon these fells show their true allegiance and proudly display their finest features to the east, and to Coniston. The most impressive single aspect, however, is that of the rock-face of Dow Crag, which is hidden from Coniston by the vast bulk of Coniston Old Man.

N
GREAT CARRS
WETHERLAM
GREY FRIAR
SWIRL HOW
Levers Water
Seathwaite Tarn
BRIM FELL
Low Water
DOW CRAG
CONISTON OLD MAN
Goats Water
Buck Pike
Brown Pike
Coniston
Road
Walna Scar
Seathwaite
Walna Scar

The Old Man is the highest fell in the group, and by far the most popular. It is one of the few lakeland fells that for a great many people is their one and only conquest, having been persuaded up its rugged slopes by rather more enthusiastic companions.

These being the highest fells in Lancashire until 1974, it follows that the Old Man was the summit of the County.

From the Fell gate, looking to Swirl How, Wetherlam (under snow) and nearer, Kennel Crag

BOO TARN to WALNA SCAR

Route

The track continues unerringly: faulty navigation here should lead to serious questions about one's rambling future. After an easy level stretch the track finally begins to climb in earnest and passes between two small rock gateways to reach a large cairn on the right. It signals the departure of a path up to Goats Water and onto the ridge between Dow Crag and Coniston Old Man. Continuing along the main path we very soon reach the fine stone structure of Cove Bridge which seems to melt effortlessly into its surroundings.

After a welcome breather by the side of the lively Torver Beck continue up the track. An initially squelchy section precedes some steeper climbing at last more akin to Lakeland, as the traditional zig-zag leads between various rock outcrops and unnecessary cairns. The rocks melt away as the gradient eases near the top of the pass, which is soon reached in an almost moorland-type setting. The tiniest of cairns marks the highest point.

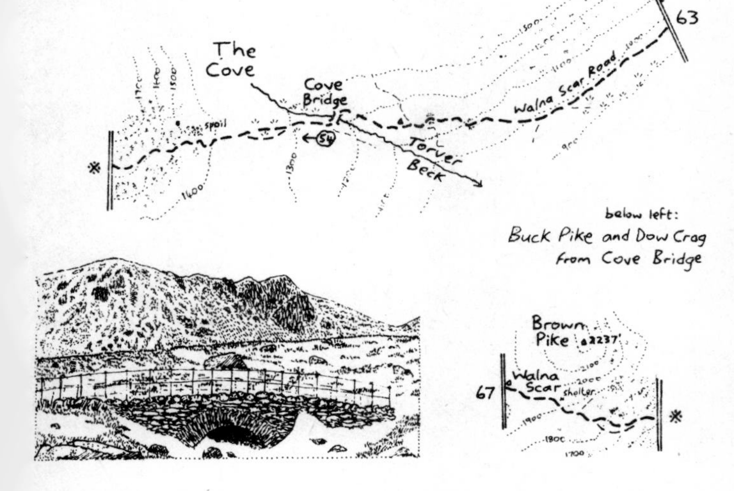

below left:
Buck Pike and Dow Crag from Cove Bridge

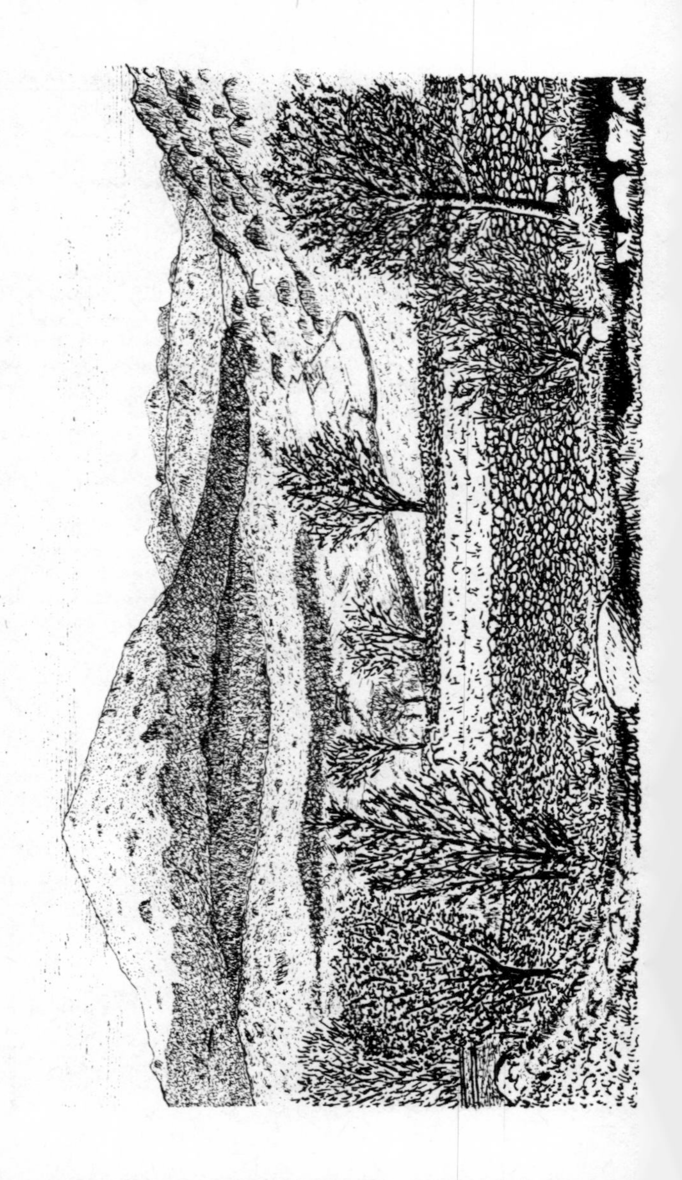

WALNA SCAR to SEATHWAITE BRIDGE

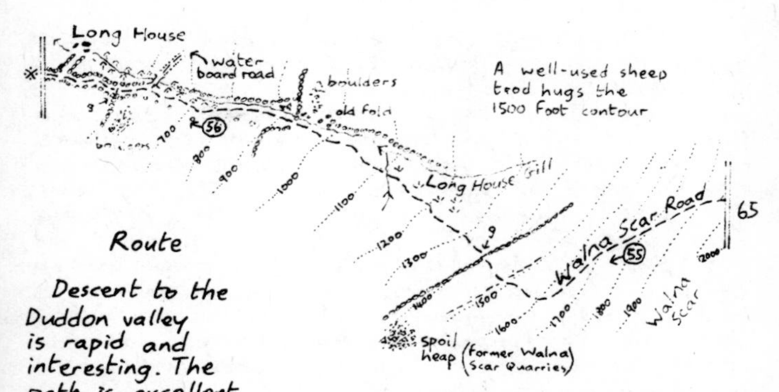

Route

Descent to the Duddon valley is rapid and interesting. The path is excellent and so are the views, the shapely Harter Fell looking particularly attractive. The track is initially very well graded and thus permits large strides. After swinging right to pass through a gate in the intake wall it then descends a little more directly alongside Longhouse Gill.

After passing through another wall the track joins a private water board road on its way down from Seathwaite Tarn. It descends past Long House Farm, across to the right, and shortly joins the narrow road that threads its way slowly up the valley.

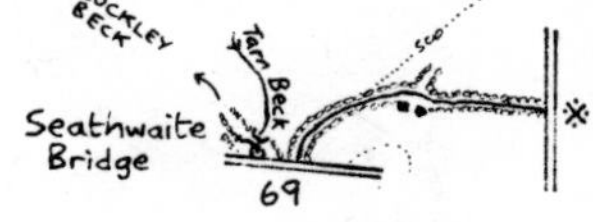

On joining the valley road note the attractive little bridge in the bottom.

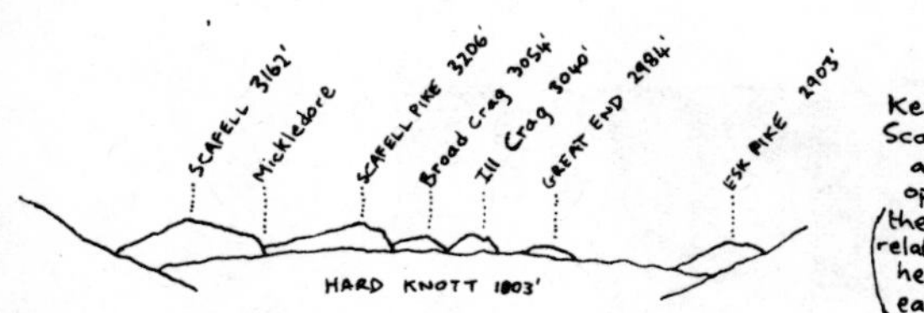

Key to the Scafell group as seen opposite (the figures relate to the heights of each summit)

left: Harter Fell and the Scafells from the water board road bridge

Route

On joining the valley road overlooking Seathwaite Bridge, follow it, a mere lane, for a gentle half-mile into Seathwaite.

After the necessary break, continue suitably refreshed on the road out of the village, but only 200 yards past the inn take a dilapidated stile on the right, signposted to the 'Stepping Stones'. The path descends through trees to negotiate Tarn Beck by means of stepping stones which are but an appetiser for the larger version to follow shortly. Turn left to accompany the beck to its confluence with the River Duddon, then turn to follow the main river upstream to arrive at the stepping stones in beautiful woodland surroundings.

Should this challenge prove a little daunting, the unenthusiastic can opt for the striking footbridge only a tiny distance further upstream. Sadly our route now forgoes Duddon's company by heading directly away from it, to leave also the woods, by means of a gate. The farm of High Wallowbarrow stands just ahead, and is reached by a path through the couple of fields in between.

Seathwaite Church

SEATHWAITE BRIDGE to WALLOWBARROW

The Duddon is a real pearl of a river, and William Wordsworth clearly thought so too, penning near three dozen sonnets in admiration. The river is born on the fells above Wrynose Pass, and soon creates a valley which happily remains narrow and fell-bound almost to its emergence into the Irish Sea, where a major estuary is formed. For the most part the river remains lively and active, the wooded environs of Tongue Wood being characteristic. Throughout its entire length it forms the old boundary between Cumberland and Furness.

Wordsworth also wrote of the Rev. Robert - Known as Wonderful - Walker, for 60 years vicar of Seathwaite, seemingly best remembered for leaving savings of £2000 from an annual stipend never exceeding £50

Wallowbarrow Crag from Seathwaite

Though little more than a hamlet Seathwaite is a most welcoming community, being the highest in the dale and directly on our route. In this most peaceful of settings with the beck nearby and the fells (in particular the impressive Wallowbarrow Crag) rising steeply above, there is a strong temptation to linger on here on a hot summer's day.

The little church of the Holy Trinity was built in 1874 and is the last resting place of the Rev. Walker (see above). A postbus service provides useful transport down to Broughton-in-Furness.

The footbridge over the Duddon, inscribed thus:-
'Built by W. Grisenthwaite
for AF and RAF
1934

Route

From the farmyard take the gate just to the right of the farmhouse and follow a track straight up the hill to pass through another gate. From it the path continues up through the bracken to reach a gate admitting to the wood. A good path zig-zags steeply through trees and bracken, but on crossing the beck emerges into the open air again. Now well above the beck, the path rises across the fell under the forbidding Wallowbarrow Crag to eventually level out amidst outcrops of heather.

A track to the hidden Stonythwaite is joined and followed to the right between small rock outcrops and more of the ubiquitous heather. The undulating track is a delight to follow and permits time to gaze with appreciation at the upper Duddon's surround of fells. On rounding one corner Harter Fell appears ahead, looking particularly impressive. This same track is followed without any difficulties to the isolated farm of Grassguards.

WALLOWBARROW to GRASSGUARDS

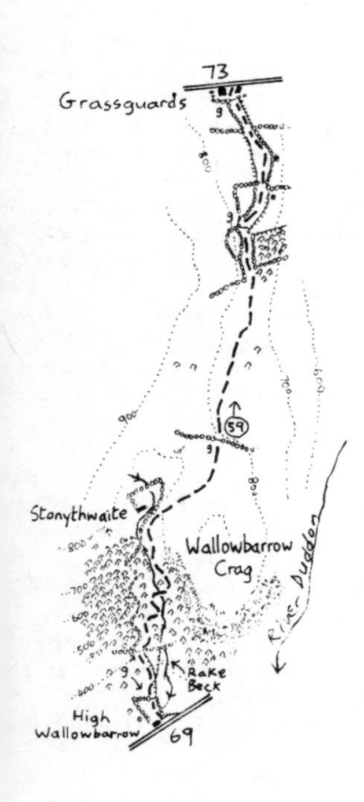

From Stonythwaite to Grassguards the path does not even attempt to climb further out of the valley, instead simply contouring across the fellside.

On climbing above the trees look back across the valley to see the shapely Caw rising above Seathwaite. It very much resembles Harter Fell, while to its right is the even more modestly-elevated Stickle Pike, which tapers to a fine peak.

Wallowbarrow Crag is at its most impressive on leaving the farmyard of High Wallowbarrow, from where it towers menacingly above.

High Wallowbarrow: a typical Lakeland farm in a truly superb setting

Route

Pass through the farmyard at Grassguards and immediately after the main building go through a gate on the left to follow the beck on the right, ignoring first a ford and then a footbridge. On rising to pass through the next gate the open fell is reached. Sadly it will not remain open fell for long, as the saplings of the Forestry Commission will inevitably envelope us in yet another of their characterless forests.

The path climbs gradually through several rather squelchy areas, which may well become drier and clearer when the trees take over (big deal!). Across to the right stands the established forest, while to the left further drainage work signals the arrival of the new one. The highlight of this prolongued uphill trek is the striking appearance across to the left of that miniature Cuillin, the rugged little hills around Green Crag. I don't wish to harp on, but...... before too long we'll be robbed of that delight.

After still more dampness underfoot, a crosswall is eventually reached, and after crossing the stile the brow of the hill really is just ahead. Unfortunately the wettest part yet is now encountered, but the sketchy path sensibly takes evasive action by crossing the beck to accompany the forest fence on the right. The trees end at the brow of the hill: here take a stile in the fence and continue in the same direction. The much-improved path crosses the undulating shoulder of Harter Fell amidst heather and bracken with constantly-improving views ahead, across Eskdale.

On reaching the second stile in the fence at a point where it parts company with the beck, cross the fence and the beck to follow a pleasant green path through the bracken. With the inviting green floor of Eskdale below, the path soon descends to the intake-wall which is followed to the left to drop to a gate. Pass through it and descend through the field to join a tractor-track, which is followed to the left to the attractive farmstead of Penny Hill.

GRASSGUARDS to PENNY HILL

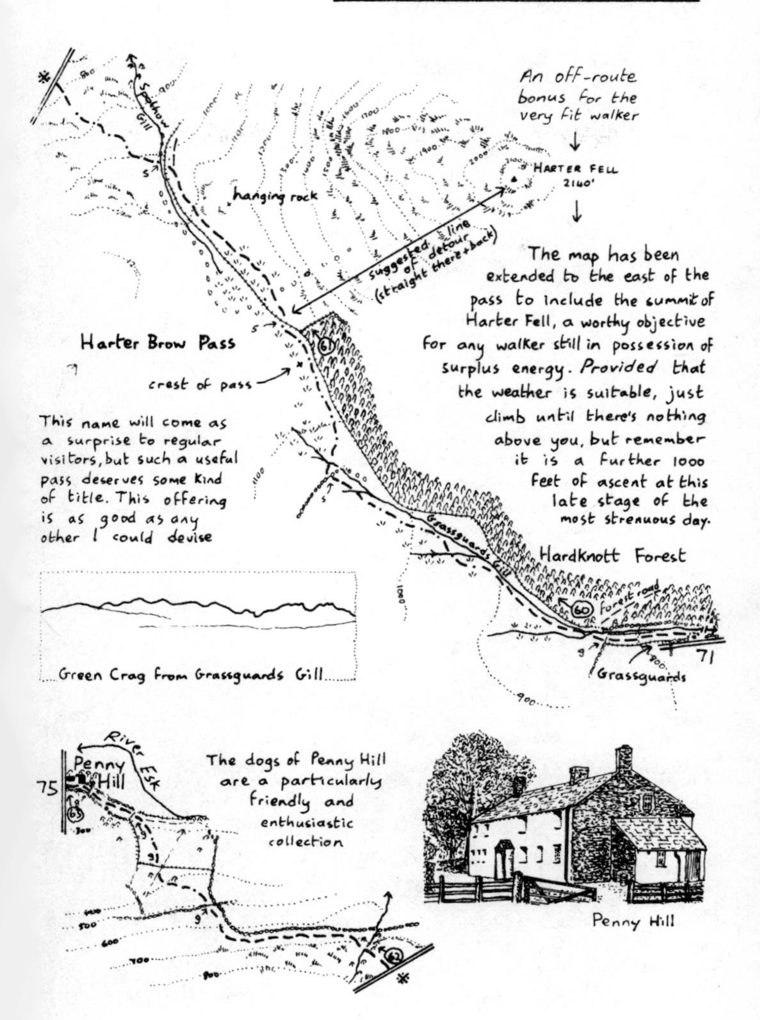

Doctor Bridge and the River Esk

The tiny village of Boot is the last community of any size in Eskdale, though itself only a tiny place. It stands just off the valley road on a short cul-de-sac lane. Around a century ago iron ore was won from the fell slopes above and taken down the valley on the railway, which at that time wasn't the narrow guage we see today. Boot's two most interesting features stand together at the head of the village. The present packhorse bridge is over 250 years old, and from it a popular walkers path leads to Wasdale Head, having once been a corpse-road from there for burial in Eskdale. By the bridge is an old corn-mill, excellently restored by the county council in 1975, and now with a working waterwheel is open to the public.

The old corn mill, Boot

PENNY HILL to BOOT

Route

Pass along the front of the farmhouse and out along the farm road to reach the small but attractive Doctor Bridge (contrary to its title it is a stone structure and not a medical person).* Use the bridge to cross the River Esk, a brief acquaintance to be much strengthened tomorrow.

Turn right along the lane which rises to debouch onto the narrow road that winds its way slowly up Eskdale. If the youth hostel is the days objective, then turn right here for a ten-minute walk along the road past the Woolpack Inn. Should Boot mark the end of the day, then stay on the route and turn left along the road for 350 yards, then turn right along a track signposted to Stony Tarn, Eel Tarn and Christcliff Farm.

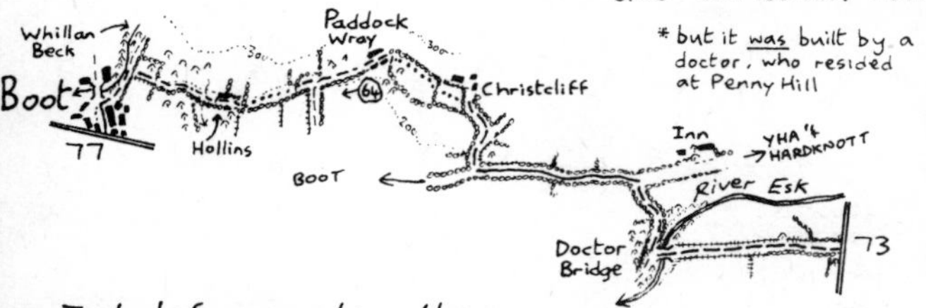

* but it was built by a doctor, who resided at Penny Hill

Just before reaching the farm buildings of Christcliff, take a gate on the left signposted to Boot. Cross the field to a stile opposite, then pass through a gate at the far right corner to enter the farmyard of Paddock Wray. Follow the farm track out at the other side and when it bends sharp left towards the road, aim straight ahead to a stile. From it continue on the level with the wall on the left to arrive through some rampant undergrowth at Hollins Farm. Leave by a gate at the far end, along a good path once again above a wall. On crossing a stile the wall is succeeded by a fence, at the end of which another stile empties onto a steep lane. Turn left to descend by Whillan Beck into Boot.

DAY SIX — BOOT TO RAVENGLASS

Distance - 10½ miles

Going - easy

Highest point - Hooker Crag, 758'

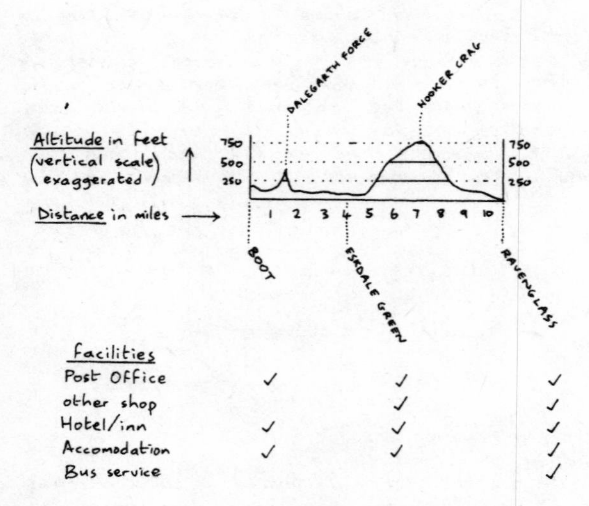

Facilities	Boot	Eskdale Green	Ravenglass
Post Office	✓	✓	✓
other shop		✓	✓
Hotel/inn	✓	✓	✓
Accomodation	✓	✓	✓
Bus service			✓

The final day provides a chance to wind down by means of an easy but highly attractive 10½ miles as the course of the River Esk is followed to the sea. After a few miles near the river - including a visit to a beautiful waterfall - the Way takes to the hills to traverse the length of Muncaster Fell. The splendour of Muncaster Castle and the Roman ruins of Walls Castle ensure interest is maintained to the very end, to the final yards along the beach and into Ravenglass.

BOOT to the RIVER ESK

Dalegarth Station is the inland terminus of the Ravenglass and Eskdale Railway. It is only two minutes walk from Boot, being visible from the crossroads. If a train is in it's well worth a little detour.

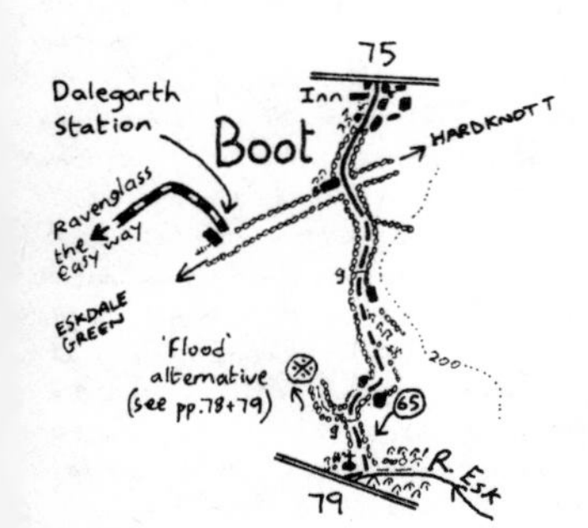

Route

Proceed down the lane, Boot's main street, to emerge back onto the road running along the valley. Go straight across and along the lane opposite which descends unerringly to the isolated church of St. Catherine in an idyllic setting by the River Esk.

St. Catherines Church

Route

Unlike the Duddon yesterday, the River Esk here does not provide an easy alternative to its stepping stones, but fortunately they are relatively simple to cross (NOTE: should the river be in such spate as to render its crossing inadvisable, then take the option marked ⊛ on the map). Assuming the opposite bank has been safely reached, turn right on a good path through bracken to enter a gate into woodland. A wooden footbridge takes us over Stanley Gill, and then a gate leads into a field at the far end of which a track is reached climbing up from Dalegarth Hall.

From here the detour to Dalegarth Force can be made. It uses up only half an hour, and is a most worthwhile exercise, more so, of course, after some rain. Turn left up the track, leaving it very shortly by a gate on the left, to enter once again the wooded environs of Stanley Gill. A delightful path now leads up alongside the beck: as the ravine narrows the beck has to be crossed three times by wooden footbridges, the last of these being the viewpoint for the falls, and the terminus of the path. Steps can now be retraced to rejoin the path above Dalegarth Hall.

A signpost points the way to Forge Bridge and a stile sets us on our way. Step-by-step instructions seem rather superfluous here, for no doubts arise that a glimpse at the map opposite won't clarify. In the latter stages the path comes nearer the river. When it emerges onto a lane alongside Forge Bridge, cross the river and head up the lane to reach the prominent and inviting whitewashed inn.

Dalegarth Hall

The RIVER ESK to the GEORGE IV INN

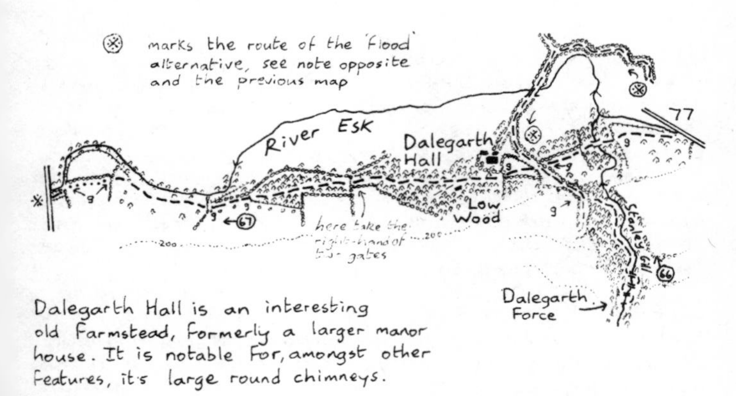

Dalegarth Hall is an interesting old farmstead, formerly a larger manor house. It is notable for, amongst other features, it's large round chimneys.

Dalegarth Force

The Esk rises as a mountain stream in the heart of England's highest mountains, the Scafell group. It descends from around 2400 feet to only 400 feet in a mere 5 miles, and remains throughout it's journey incredibly clear and sparkling.

Our acquaintance with the river coincides with it's passage between richly wooded banks and green pastures. Within the bounds of the valley, the Esk gives it's name to a village, a railway and a near-3000 foot peak.

81
BOOT
HARDKNOTT
Inn
barn
River Esk
farm
68
Milkingstead Wood
Forge Bridge
RAVENGLASS
WABERTHWAITE

Route

After partaking of any necessary refreshment continue up the road behind the inn towards Eskdale Green. Just before the road bridges the railway line, leave it along an enclosed bridlepath to the left immediately adjacent to the entrance to Eskdale Green's tidy little station. On eventually passing through a stile by a gate, the track stays with the wall on the left to avoid a host of over-enthusiastic bushes. When free of them it loses itself in the large field: bear to the top right corner to leave by a broken fence.

Pass to the right of a prominent little upthrust of trees and rocks to cross a stile in a fence and enter a large expanse of rough pasture. A good path now crosses our route but is of no use to us, so head straight across the pasture to meet the fence coming across from the left. On nearing the wall ahead, pass through a gate in the fence to reach a gate in the wall itself. From it the path begins the gradual climb up the fellside to shortly pass through another gate before continuing upward.

The gradient soon eases and up on the skyline to the right a strange lunar-like object appears. This T.V. signal receiver is well worth the heathery scramble thereto, not for its own interest (which is little to us, if not to the residents of Eskdale) but for the fact that the cairn atop Silver Knott is only yards to the right.

George IV
Eskdale Green

The GEORGE IV INN to SILVER KNOTT

The 'River Mite'

Though Eskdale Green proper is not entered, the little station can be seen just before leaving the road.

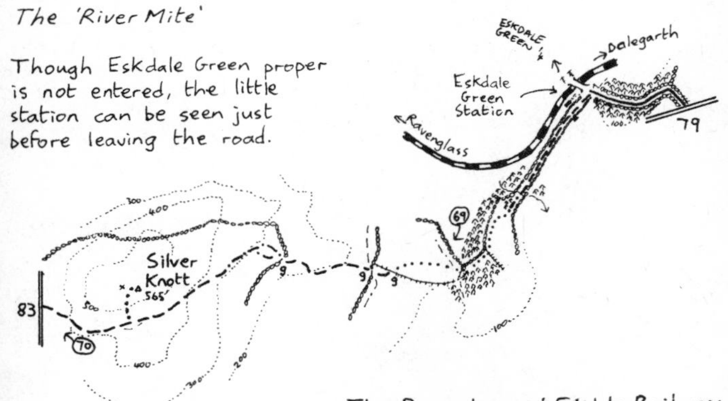

The Ravenglass and Eskdale Railway was opened in 1875 to transport iron ore from the mines in Eskdale to the main line at Ravenglass. In no time at all it was also carrying passengers. From the demise of that particular venture to it's acquisition by a preservation society in the early 1960's, it had a chequered history, being opened and closed numerous times. and almost disappearing completely. Today of course it is a highly successful operation, and thousands travel on this narrow-guage line, known as 'La'al Ratty' each year, one of the several steam engines usually being in action.

Looking north to the Illgill Head ridge and Scafell

On Hooker Crag

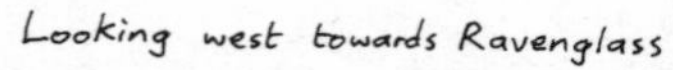

Looking west towards Ravenglass

Route

On regaining the main path continue along the fell: this clear, undulating trail is a delight to tread as it weaves through the bracken. On passing through a gate by a wall corner the path encounters a slightly marshy section before climbing to reach the small table-like group of stones collectively known as Ross's Camp. The level top-stone makes a splendid perch amidst the heather, from which to survey the journey's end.

As the path carries on it retains the excellent views of lower Eskdale. Another marsh is skirted before the path forks; take the right one to climb steeply and rapidly to the trig. point on Hooker Crag.

81
Muncaster Fell
71
Ross's Camp
Hooker Crag
758
85
700
600
500
400

Hooker Crag is surmounted by a rugged little upthrust of rocks that serve to confirm it's superiority over the rest of Muncaster Fell.

Ross's Camp bearing it's name and the year 1883, apparently the handiwork of a shooting party.

Muncaster Castle

is an enormous sandstone structure enclosed by some beautiful grounds renowned for their rhododendron display. The house began life like others we have seen, as a 14th century pele tower, and the building we see today is mostly little more than a century old. It has been in the possession of the Lords of Muncaster, the Pennington Family since the days of the pele tower, and these days can be shared briefly by the public. Inside are beautiful portraits and furniture while outside is also a bird garden.

We are most fortunate that a right of way crosses through these normally restricted grounds, and with just a short stray from the path, much more of the Castle can be seen.

The lych-gate, Muncaster Church

The Church of St. Michael stands within the grounds of the castle, in a lovely secluded corner of it's own, enclosed in greenery

Muncaster Castle, west front

HOOKER CRAG to MUNCASTER CASTLE

Route

Vacate Hooker Crag by means of the path which appears to be making a bee-line for Ravenglass. It drops down to rejoin the main path across the fell, the open fellside shortly giving way to enclosed woodland. Already the influence of Muncaster Castle is strong, in the park-like surroundings of rhodedendron bushes and a fine variety of trees. The path is by now a wide track, and brings us down rapidly to the A595 at a sharp bend.

If Ravenglass must be reached desperately quickly, head straight down the A595. This uninspiring finish should however be invoked as a very last resort only.

A left turn along the main road leads to a drive into the otherwise firmly-enclosed grounds of Muncaster Castle. Cross the road and head down the drive, the first object of interest being the church. On joining another track with the bird garden on the right and the Castle across to the left, a series of footpath signs guide us across a lawn and past a duckpond to join another track. This is followed to the left for only a short distance before heading up a narrower path which forks right through the trees. A most enjoyable woodland walk now ensues.

gaps in the trees afford a brief glimpse back to the Castle

Walls Castle

Many centuries ago Ravenglass was a port of much importance. Used as such by the Romans, who built a fort here - Glannaventa - on which now stands Walls Mansion. Of most interest now are the remains of Walls Castle, thought to have been a bath-house of the Romans. Ravenglass also had one of Cumbria's first markets, in 1208.

Ravenglass is the end of the road, and as if to emphasise this point it's main street continues as far as possible before literally dropping onto the beach. Although it is fairly and squarely on the coast, Ravenglass is sheltered from the worst excesses of the weather due to the indentations of the coastline. Although only as dunes, land reaches out another mile further west in the form of the two outer arms of the estuaries of the rivers Irt and Esk. Immediately in front of Ravenglass they join forces with the smaller River Mite, and together head out to sea as the River Esk. Nowhere else on the Cumbrian coast does such a situation occur, and because of the natural history hereabouts, the extensive dunes are a nature reserve.

The village consists only of it's main street along the front, and the environs of the Ravenglass and Eskdale Railway, which of course has its headquarters here. Were it not in fact for the railway, then the place would be very quiet indeed. Ravenglass itself has not cashed in on the visitors, and next to it Arnside almost resembles Blackpool. Despite being warned by a chap on Hooker Crag that it was the most inhospitable place he had ever visited, it is the simple peacefulness that is attractive and - as long as it's not raining - it is an ideally-relaxing location to conclude our walk.

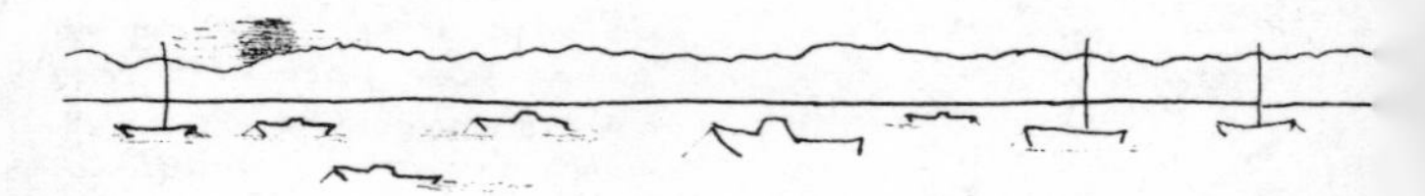

MUNCASTER CASTLE to RAVENGLASS

Route

Shortly after the trees begin to thin out, a wall is reached. After scratching your head at the sudden disappearance of an excellent path, leave the gate by heading south-west across a large expanse of open parkland, aiming to the left of the woods hiding Ravenglass from sight. A gateway in an old fence will soon be located, and from there a sketchy trod leads to a step-stile in a fence. Descend through a small new plantation-which appears to leave little room for a footpath- to the prominent buildings at Newtown. Keep to the right of their enclosed grounds to join the access drive by means of a gate in the fence ahead.

Follow the drive to the right to arrive at a junction in front of the impressive-looking Walls Mansion.

A right turn leads to the ruins of Walls Castle. After a brief inspection continue along the drive for a short distance to locate a path branching left under a railway bridge and onto the beach. Ravenglass is at last visible, and within two minutes it is reached.

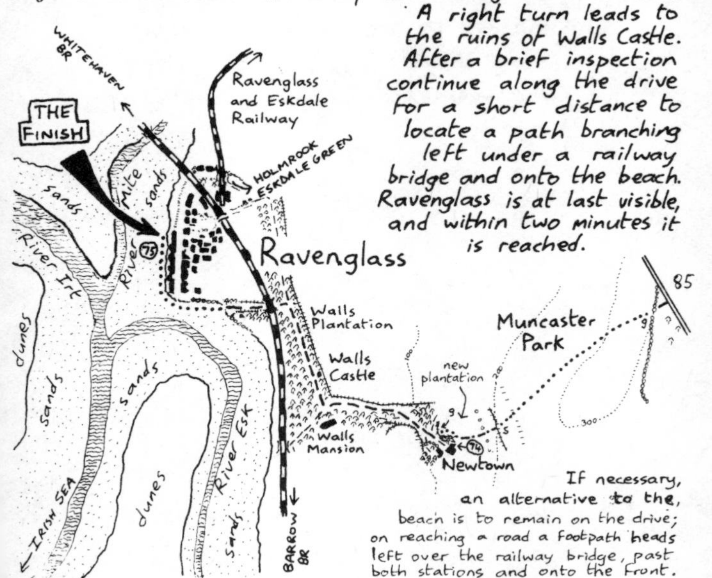

If necessary, an alternative to the beach is to remain on the drive; on reaching a road a footpath heads left over the railway bridge, past both stations and onto the front.

The following five pages are intended to provide a permanent record of the Way, for the walker who wishes to complete them.

RECORD OF ACCOMODATION

Below are enough spaces to record all the overnight stops used on the walk, from the rat-infested barn to the overnight boot-clean service

Date	Address	Comments

RECORD OF THE JOURNEY

This and the opposite page enable a permanent record of the walk to be kept

Date	Place	Miles		Times		Comments
		Daily	Total	Arrival	Departure	
	Arnside	—	—			
	Hazelslack	1¾	1¾			
	Haverbrack	3½	3½			
	Milnthorpe	4½	4½			
	Heversham	5¾	5¾			
	Sizergh Castle	9½	9½			
	Helsington Church	10¾	10¾			
	Brigsteer	11½	11½			
	Crosthwaite	15	15			
	Lords Seat, Whitbarrow	3½	18½			
	Witherslack Hall	4½	19½			
	Witherslack Church	6	21			
	River Winster	7¾	22¾			
	Lindale	9¾	24¾			
	Hampsfell	11½	26½			
	Cartmel	13	28			
	Howbarrow	2	30			
	Bigland Tarn	4¾	32¾			
	Low Wood	5¾	33¾			

Date	Place	Miles		Times		Comments
		Daily	Total	Arrival	Departure	
	Greenodd	8	36			
	Spark Bridge	10½	38½			
	Lowick Green	11¼	39¼			
	Lowick Bridge	12½	40½			
	Stock	2	42½			
	Arnsbarrow Hill	4	44½			
	Top O'Selside	5	45½			
	Grizedale Forest	6½	47			
	Lawson Park	8	48½			
	Waterhead	10	50½			
	Coniston	11	51½			
	Boo Tarn	1½	53			
	Walna Scar Pass	3¼	54¾			
	Seathwaite Bridge	5¼	56¾			
	Seathwaite	5¾	57¼			
	Grassguards	8¼	59¾			
	Penny Hill	11½	63			
	Boot	13	64½			
	St. Catherines Church	½	65			
	King George IV Inn	3¾	68¼			
	Hooker Crag	7	71½			
	Muncaster Castle	8½	73			
	Ravenglass	10½	75			

RECORD OF HOTELS AND INNS VISITED

Both these pages are provided so that a note may be kept of any hostelries that are inspected during the course of the walk. An entry on every line is not obligatory.

Date	Inn	Location	Beers sampled	Comments

Date	Inn	Location	Beers sampled	Comments

INDEX OF PLACE NAMES ON THE ROUTE MAPS

INDEX continued

INDEX continued